Gold

THE MAKING OF *BAND OF GOLD* AND THE SEQUEL *GOLD*

Anthony Hayward

CHAMELEON

in association with Granada Television

First published in Great Britain
in 1997 by Chameleon Books,
an imprint of André Deutsch Ltd
106 Great Russell Street
London WC1B 3LJ

www.vci.co.uk

André Deutsch is a subsidiary of VIC plc

Published in association with Granada Television

Printed and bound in Great Britain by Butler and Tanner, Frome and London

A catalogue record for this book is available from the British Library

ISBN 0 233 99048 8

Editorial and design by
Brown Packaging Books Ltd
Bradley's close
74–77 White Lion Street
London N1 9PF

Contents

Introduction

Prostitutes walk the streets of Bradford plying their trade. A young housewife and mother, who has split from her violent husband, goes on the game to pay off her debts after being threatened by a loan shark. She takes to the Lane in a skimpy, black dress, and is shown the ropes by a single mother who makes ends meet by selling her body. And when the first woman solicits alone, she is driven to a remote spot and murdered. A serial killer is on the loose and all those in the red-light district of Bradford live in fear.

This is the story that launched ITV's *Band of Gold* in 1995. Far from being sensationalist and titillating, it was a gritty drama about the lives of women working on the streets in the north of England. Some television industry insiders were worried that it might be too unglamorous, but *Band of Gold* gripped British television viewers immediately. More than 15 million tuned in regularly to the six-part serial, making it the most popular programme on British tele-vision in 1995 – apart from *Coronation Street*. And after its screening in America, readers of *Time* magazine voted it the fifth-best programme on TV.

The serial also catapulted its writer, Kay Mellor, to fame, making her one of television's biggest success stories of the 1990s. The story of *Band of Gold* is as much about Kay as the characters featured in her scripts: they come from the heart, for Kay grew up in a working-class area of Leeds and married at 16 after becoming pregnant – 'It won't last,' the vicar said on her wedding day. But, almost 30 years later, she is still with her husband, Anthony. Kay found her vocation in acting and writing, and much of her work as a writer has focused on relationships and the dilemmas that individuals face.

Many people have helped me in my research for this book and I would like to thank the following: Kay Mellor; her assistant, Linda Neary; *Gold* Producer Gill McNeill; Executive Producer Gub Neal; Production Designer Chris Wilkinson; Costume Designer Ray Holman; Make-up Designer Sue Milton; Casting Director Carolyn Bartlett; Stunt Arranger Stuart St Paul; Publicity Officer Mariette Masters; and actresses Geraldine James, Cathy Tyson and Janet Dibley, and actors Danny Edwards and Colin Salmon. Thanks are also due to the following, who worked on *Band of Gold*: Executive Producer Sally Head; Producer Tony Dennis; Director Richard Standeven; Costume Designers Sue Peck and Nic Ede; actresses Ruth Gemmell and Barbara Dickson; and actor Ray Stevenson. I would also like to thank Nicky Paris and Deborah Waight at André Deutsch, and Elaine Collins and Lisa McKay at WCA for their support, and Deborah, my wife.

Anthony Hayward

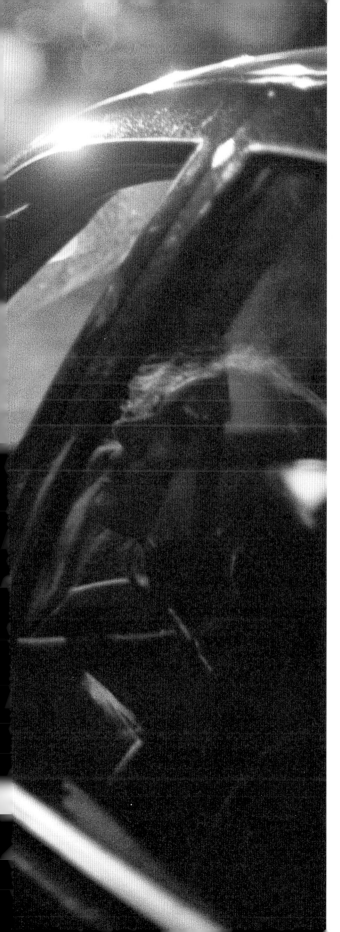

1

A Winter's Tale

One winter's evening in November 1989, writer and actress Kay Mellor was picked up by her husband from the National Children's Home Care Line office in Leeds – she did voluntary work there once a week as a counsellor, taking telephone calls from children who had been sexually abused or were in distress, putting those in desperate need in touch with therapists, and giving advice to parents who were under threat of having their gas or electricity cut off. The couple set off for a party in Bradford, but they took a wrong turning that was to change Kay's life.

'By mistake we drove up Lumb Lane, which is a notorious red-light area,' recalls Kay. 'I could see a young girl and immediately thought: "She's a prostitute." Our car had tinted windows, so she couldn't see that there was a woman inside. She stepped forward and bobbed down to look into the

Gina (Ruth Gemmell) solicits for business in the first episode of *Band of Gold*

Haunted by the memory of a 'sweetie girl' called Tracy, aged just 13 or 14, Kay Mellor created
Band of Gold and schoolgirl runaway Tracy Richards (Samantha Morton)

car to see if there was a potential punter, but when she realized I was a woman she stepped back. She could only have been 13 or 14 and had blonde hair, a denim jacket, a crop top, a leather mini-skirt and white high-heeled shoes that must have been crippling her. Her legs were bare – they were completely blue and mottled with the cold. She still had a baby face and hadn't lost her puppy fat. I just remember being completely shocked, because I had daughters her age. I felt as if someone had just punched me in the stomach and winded me.

'As we drove on to the party, I didn't know whether to continue or to go back and say something. But I thought: "What are you going to say if you go back?" – so we drove on to the party. And it was the worst one I have ever been to in my life, because all I could think of was the young girl standing out there on the Lane, prostituting herself. "Whose daughter is she? Whose sister is she? Who is she?" I kept thinking.

'And I was still thinking about it the following Thursday, when I went back to the Care Line office. My co-ordinator, Linda Whittaker, sensed that something was on my mind, and asked if I was all right. I admitted I was worrying about something, and she asked me what I was writing. I said: "I don't know. I'm really confused and thinking of giving it all up." Then I told her about the young girl in Lumb Lane. "It's terrible," I said. "What are we doing? We've got girls of that age as prostitutes. You expect prostitutes to be 20-something." "Why don't you write about it?" said Linda.'

And that was the start of a process that culminated six years later when *Band of Gold* hit the television screens and portrayed 'the oldest profession' in a completely new light: not as 'tarts with hearts', or subjects for comedy, but as women who took to the streets as a last resort – sometimes to feed their children – and teenagers who had been abused,

who were running away from home and looking for a means of survival. It also depicted the fear with which many prostitutes have to live, always being in danger from both their clients and their pimps. The programme was a landmark in drama serials, winning the same popularity and critical acclaim as *Prime Suspect* and *Cracker*, both of which were also made by Granada Television.

It was an enormous achievement for Kay Mellor, who, with her brother, was brought up single-handedly by her mother on a council estate in Leeds, then married husband Anthony when she was just 16 and had two daughters: Gaynor, who joined *Coronation Street* to play Judy Mallett in 1995, and Yvonne. 'I had left school to do a typing course, and then I got pregnant and married Anthony,' Kay recalls. 'But as the kids got older, I didn't know what to do. So I went to college and collected O- and A-levels – I can't remember how many. I just had a huge thirst for knowledge and couldn't quench it. I loved learning and became obsessed with it. Then, when I was doing an A-level in drama at Park Lane College, in Leeds, Gordon Wright, a tutor, asked me to read for the part of Viola in *Twelfth Night*. After he'd heard me, he said: "Has anyone ever told you that you should be an actress?" So I went to Bretton Hall, in Wakefield, as a mature student – it's a drama college affiliated to Leeds University.' It was a good choice, because celebrated playwrights John Godber and Colin Welland are both ex-students of Bretton Hall.

Kay was 26 when she started the full-time course and when she left, three years later, she founded the Yorkshire Theatre Company with two friends: they drove around the country in a transit van and performed in theatres, pubs, youth clubs, prisons and psychiatric units. As well as acting, she wrote plays. The first one to be performed was

> *'I had daughters her age. I felt as if someone had just punched me in the stomach and winded me'*

Paul, about a mentally handicapped boy, which was written while she was still at drama school – it was nominated as best new play in the National Students' Drama Festival. This success inspired Kay's husband, Anthony, to give up the small garage he owned and train to look after people with learning difficulties. The couple made a pact that Kay would become the bread-winner – just as Anthony had previously taken on the role to keep the family afloat. Anthony has since become a social worker and now runs a day-care centre.

Then another of Kay's plays, *Climbing Out*, was adapted for the screen by Yorkshire Television. Her first, brief TV appearance as an actress was as Dr Baker in the Granada Television series *The Practice*, after which she landed the role of PC Kershaw in the same company's soap, *Albion Market*, in 1985.

'I wrote a script for *Albion Market* on spec, shoved it in a brown envelope at the Granada reception and it ended up on executive producer Bill Podmore's desk,' remembers Kay. 'He arranged to meet me and said: "You're a great writer," and asked whether I wanted to act or write. I knew I could act, but at that time I just wanted to write: it was so exciting to me to write all of something, not just act a bit of it. There was no room for writers then, but I became a story associate on *Albion Market*. By the time they *did* need more writers, the programme was about to be taken off screen.'

Nevertheless, the fact *Climbing Out* had been well received prompted Keith Richardson, Yorkshire Television's controller of drama, to invite Kay to write a play about the effects of child-abuse accusations on a family. The result was *A Place of Safety*, which was nominated for the Prix Italia. Then, after writing for *Brookside* and *Coronation Street*, and creating both *Children's Ward* and *Families*, Kay had another success with three series of the

'I wasn't interested in writing a drama series so much as in finding out who the girl was and seeing if I could help'

Yorkshire Television children's drama *Just Us*, which received awards from both the Royal Television Society and the Writer's Guild. She also had a West End stage hit with the comedy *A Passionate Woman*, starring Stephanie Cole. Directed by Ned Sherrin, it was based on the life of her mother, Dinah Harris, who, in her seventies, has started writing herself, mainly drawing on her experiences in Leeds earlier this century.

But Kay's biggest success was still to come: six years after the evening in 1989 that continued to haunt her and which had led her, at the time, to research and write *Band of Gold*. Together with Linda Whittaker, from the Care Line office in Leeds, she visited the Manningham area of Bradford in an attempt to find the teenage prostitute whom she had seen a week earlier. 'We were driven by an ex-policewoman friend of Linda's,' she recalls. 'To be honest, I wasn't interested in writing a drama series so much as in finding out who the young girl was and seeing what I could do to help her. I'm sure that I had found her that day, *Band of Gold* would never have been written.

'When I spoke to other prostitutes there, I was told: "Oh, we think you mean Tracy. She went to Birmingham." Apparently, she had pimp problems and left. That's the nearest I ever got to finding out about her. From that snippet, I developed Tracy's story in *Band of Gold*. I even went to Birmingham a month later, but never found her. I asked if anyone knew Tracy from Leeds and was told: "There are thousands of Tracys here, love." A lot of prostitutes are called Tracy or Sharon – they're just pseudonyms. So I never found her, but I spoke to a lot of people in Birmingham about prostitution. I met a young housewife who went on the game after getting into debt and her husband didn't know about it: that's what inspired me to write the story of Gina, in episode one.

'On the same visit, I also went to see a producer at BBC Pebble Mill, Hilary Salmon, who had asked me what I wanted to write next after *A Place of Safety*. I said that I was planning a drama about why women went into prostitution. The BBC commissioned it as a four-part series and then I started to research the subject properly.'

Returning to Lumb Lane, in Bradford, Kay sought out prostitutes who could provide her with the material she needed to write a programme that would accurately reflect the everyday realities of life on the game. Her research took many months. 'I had to understand everything about being a prostitute,' says Kay. 'The language is quite different: they say "trick pads" where I would say "brothels"; and "rubbers" where I would say "condoms". They talk about "ponces", "blow jobs" and "hand jobs", "no mouth" and how much it costs for it all. You

The characters of those who formed the band in *Band of Gold* – played by Barbara Dickson and Cathy Tyson (back), Geraldine James and Samantha Morton (front) – were thoroughly researched by Kay Mellor

Gina (Ruth Gemmell) was a mixture of a housewife whom Kay Mellor met in Birmingham, who went on the game after getting into debt, and a single parent who worked on Lumb Lane after seeing a friend make money by doing so have to learn all that and discover how they actually feel about it, and understand their personal sexuality. There's a myth that prostitutes enjoy sex, but, in fact, part of their act is to persuade clients that they are enjoying it. Most of them don't get any pleasure out of it at all. It's a job – they clock in and clock out.

'I soon found out there was a hierarchy on the Lane. I was going around asking young girls to talk to me and was told I should go to the pub. So I went there with Linda and Liz, the ex-police-woman, and everyone looked at us, which was a bit worrying. Then, this woman came over to me and said: "So what do they call you?" I told her who I was and said I was researching into prostitution, which sounded such a naff thing to say. She said: "If you want to know anything about the Lane, you come through me." I was bloody terrified! She was a big woman. At the time, I assumed it was to do with money – but it was actually about hierarchy. You went through her and she put you in touch with whoever you wanted.'

That pub was called the Dutton Arms – it is a chemist's shop now – and it provided the inspiration for the Hustler's Arms in Kay's story. And Christine became the role model for Rose Garrity in the series.

'That was my first meeting with Christine,' says Kay. She started to paint a picture of what life was like on the Lane. She said: "I run the Lane. Nobody goes on my patch. I know who stands where and nobody does it without a rubber – if anyone did, I'd beat their head in." She also told me about "sweetie girls": the under-age prostitutes who do it for just a fiver.

'Christine was bright and in her late thirties – hence the story about Rose going to college. Christine was also very interesting because her husband was serving life for murder, and she had gone on to the streets to feed her two kids, one of

'I run the Lane...I know who stands where and nobody does it without a rubber'

whom wasn't very well. She couldn't manage on benefits, but couldn't work because she had to look after the children. And she only went out on the streets when she had to.

'She told me a lot of this during our first meeting – and she had the three of us sussed immediately. Turning to each of us, she said, "You're a sort of social worker; you're an ex-copper; and you're different." It was just her nous – these women live by their wits. I told her I was a writer – not a journalist, a police-man or a documentary-maker, but a playwright. I was just dead honest with her, and she was with me.'

As well as meeting Christine, Kay talked to a 'big and black' prostitute called Sonia – a single parent with two children. She had once worked in an off-licence during the day, but gave up that job after firing her baby-sitter, who had been stealing from her, and she couldn't get anyone else to look after the children. Sonia decided to go on the Lane after seeing that one of her friends made a living by doing so. When one of them went out, the other looked after all of their children.

'Every prostitute I met gave me something different,' recalls Kay. 'But I needed a big story, and I knew I needed to spend a lot of time with some-body to dig hard and understand the psychology of being a prostitute. Linda said she knew someone who was in therapy and trying to give up prostitu-tion, and she would give this person my telephone number. She put her job on the line doing that.

'As a result, Trea – that's not her real name – rang me and I went to her house in Leeds. What struck me first was that it was immaculately clean, with everything so polished and cared for – she was a fanatical cleaner. There's a scene in *Band of Gold* where Carol says: "I expect you thought we lived in a slum, didn't you?" That was exactly what Trea said to me at our initial meeting. I told her that the house was lovely.

'But she was very defensive, having been through a major crisis. I think that she had suffered a breakdown as a result of long-term sexual abuse: child abuse; pimp abuse; everything. She never actually told me how the breakdown manifested itself, but, when *Band of Gold* was broadcast and Carol suffered the same thing, Trea told me: "You must have got right inside my head." She had a cleaning fetish, like Carol. All the time she was talking to me about her life, she was cleaning.

'Trea had been brought up in a culture of prostitution. Early on, she was abused by her mother's boyfriends, and she went to clubs where pimps looked out for innocent, susceptible young girls. She was shockingly young when she went on the game, probably only 13 or 14.' It was the first of about 30 meetings that Kay had with Trea – and some of the stories about her experiences of abuse and how she worried about her daughter left Kay in tears.

By now, Kay had the makings of the characters who were to feature in *Band of Gold* – though originally she named the series *Frontline*. The young girl whom she had first seen in Bradford's Lumb Lane was the inspiration for 'sweetie girl' Tracy Richards, who appeared sketchily in episode one before emerging more prominently through her involvement with the other women; ageing hooker Rose Garrity was based on Christine; cleaning-obsessed Carol was the Trea figure; and debt-ridden mother Gina was a mixture of Sonia and the woman whom Kay met in Birmingham.

'Trea suffered from long-term sexual abuse – child abuse, pimp abuse, everything'

Anita, however – the madam who rents out her spare bedroom to prostitutes while being kept by her married lover – was partly inspired by someone whom Kay had met at an Ann Summers party. 'Anita thought she was one better than a prostitute,' says Kay. 'When I was thinking about writing a play about the women who go to Ann Summers parties, I gatecrashed one and it was hilarious. The demonstrator took herself deadly seriously and I creased up with laughter.

'Producing a negligée, she said: "And, for all you ladies who want a new freezer, here is the perfect thing." What she was saying was, if you want your husband to buy you a new freezer, here's the exchange rate – because when you're wearing this negligée you can have anything you want in the world. Now, if that isn't prostitution, I don't know what is. That woman obviously thought she was a cut above the rest and would have been hugely insulted if anyone had suggested that this was prostitution in its most basic form. But, in fact, she was prepared to make money out of sex, in the same way as Anita.'

In the first series of *Band of Gold*, the prostitutes lived in fear after the murder of Gina and the death of a prostitute who resembled Carol. But it was only after writing the series that Kay realized how much she had been influenced by living in Leeds at the time when the Yorkshire Ripper was stalking the City's streets. One of Peter Sutcliffe's victims, Jacqueline Hill, was murdered only a short drive from her house, and Trea and other prostitutes were all scared when they plied their trade during that period.

'All the women in the area felt vulnerable,' recalls Kay. 'Men that I knew were taken in by the police for questioning, and no woman could ever feel safe alone. I couldn't walk down the street at night, open my door or sit out in my garden. Everyone around was in a state of constant fear and panic. I don't think anybody really understands that, unless they've lived through it. It robbed me of my liberty at a time when I was into feminism and liberation. And there was such an atmosphere of hysterical suspicion. People were saying that they knew a man who had been away or out of the country and just returned. My husband even said: "I hope I'm not having blackouts

The inspiration for Carol (Cathy Tyson), who had a cleaning fetish, was a prostitute called Trea, who invited Kay Mellor into her house with the words, 'I expect you thought we lived in a slum, didn't you?'

and going out and murdering people." People were shopping each other, saying they believed they knew who the killer was.'

For Kay, *Frontline* – as the series was still called – became the most important television programme that she had ever scripted. What most concerned her was that she should keep faith with those who had helped with the research. 'I said to Trea: "You must let me give you some money for all the time you have given me,"' Kay recalls. 'She replied: "No, but I want you to do one thing for me. I want you to write it like it is. I'm sick to death of watching television and seeing some old slag in the background. And that's how prostitutes are portrayed. It makes me sick." I

remember walking away from her house, getting into my car and thinking: "I hope to God I can do that." I thought that if I just achieve one thing, it should be to point out that these people are women first and prostitutes second. They have mothers, kids and school meals to worry about.'

Fired with enthusiasm, Kay delivered one script every six weeks to BBC Pebble Mill until all four were finished. They were well received, but, even so, the BBC never put *Frontline* into production. Kay says: 'I would catch Alan Yentob, controller of BBC1, at awards ceremonies and say: "My name's Kay Mellor. You've got some scripts on your desk. You've got to make the series because it's really important." But they never did.'

2

The Band Played On...

Shortly before the BBC's option on *Frontline* ran out in November 1993, Kay Mellor took her scripts to Granada Television. David Liddiment, its programme controller, had previously been executive producer of *Coronation Street*, and was a friend of Kay's. He read the scripts, reacted enthusiastically, and passed them to the company's controller of drama, Sally Head. And both Sally and script associate Gwenda Bagshaw were immediately won over.

'We both fell in love with the scripts,' recalls Sally. 'They had an originality and a voice that had not been heard before, as well as characters we had not come across. All we had seen on television in this vein previously were "tarts with hearts". These scripts dug into them as human beings and weren't patronizing towards them. Also, as well as being moving, the series was

Rose's journey to London was followed in detail when *Frontline* was expanded and retitled

More screen time allowed Kay Mellor to explore the grief of Gina's mother, Joyce (Rachel Davies)

more of Joyce's grief after the death of her daughter, Gina. We were able to follow Rose and Tracy going to London, too. In the original, we weren't able to go with them. We also followed Carol to the psychiatric centre after she had her breakdown.'

Kay had to finish writing the series in time for filming in the late summer of 1994, with transmission planned for early the following year. 'The scripts for episodes five and six were completed just two weeks before the read-through in advance of filming,' recalls Sally. For Kay, one of the most difficult things of all was to convey what the series was really about to those working on it. 'It was quite traumatic,' she remembers, 'because no one knew what the vision was other than me. Everyone could understand the police aspects of the story, because they had seen *Prime Suspect* and *Cracker*. But, when it came to prostitutes, nobody had anything to grasp hold of, because there had been nothing like this before – they were into unknown territory. So I was forever telling people what things were like.'

By this time, *Frontline* had been renamed *Band of Gold*: the title refers not just to the group of women created by Kay, but also to the wedding ring worn by Gina and the fact that gold is a commodity to be sold – as are women's bodies.

Tony Dennis, who had previously worked on Granada Television's hospital drama *Medics*, became producer of the new series after Sally Head gave him a script to read in December 1993. He showed the same enthusiasm for it as she did. 'It was an exciting script,' he says. 'It vividly portrayed a grim world with an embattled group of women trying to raise their families and earn a crust in a forbidding northern city. Kay's working-class characters were not to be pitied or patronized. They were hookers and mothers, fighters and survivors of a casual,

terribly funny. It had all the ingredients that make for good television.'

Filled with enthusiasm, Sally submitted *Frontline* as a programme idea to the ITV Network Centre, whose controller of drama, Vernon Lawrence, commissioned a six-part series within three weeks. This meant some frantic activity for Kay, who had to rewrite much of the original four episodes. 'Sally wanted exactly the same story, but she said to let it breathe a bit more,' recalls Kay. 'It definitely made it better, because I could explore things in more depth. Tracy's character started to come to life, with the story of her middle-class background and her going home to confront her mother about how she was abused by her father. I was able to show

'Sally wanted exactly the same story, but she said to let it breathe a bit more. It definitely made it better'

relentless and brutalizing trade: prostitution.

'When Sally asked me if I wanted to be the producer, I was in no doubt that I had to do it. It was very rare for a project like *Band of Gold* to be given the green light. This wasn't a hospital or a cop show – it was something distinctive about real people and real issues, some of them stretching back to the very beginning of relationships between the sexes.'

Casting

One of the most important tasks that had to be undertaken before filming could begin was the casting of the lead characters: Rose, Carol, Anita, Tracy and Gina. 'I always wanted Cathy Tyson to play Carol,' says Kay. 'She looks very similar to Trea, on whom she was based. Although Cathy had played a prostitute in *Mona Lisa*, I had also seen her in the theatre and felt she was just right. There's an energy about Trea and she's hyperactive, so the actress had to be thin, have lots of energy and be beautiful in an exotic way. Now, who's going to play that part? Remember, I knew what was down the other end – that she was going to

Barbara Dickson (Anita), Geraldine James (Rose), Samantha Morton (Tracy) and Cathy Tyson (Carol) became the ensemble cast throughout the first and second series of Band of Gold

Gina, the debt-ridden mother who leaves her violent husband to team up with Carol on the streets, was the most difficult role to cast, but Ruth Gemmell (left) landed it after reading a scene with Ray Stevenson, who played husband Steve

have a breakdown. The actress would have to be brilliant and be daring enough to go on that emotional journey. A lot of actresses look right but can't quite pull it off. I spoke very loudly and clearly about who I wanted for the role.'

When Carolyn Bartlett became casting director on *Band of Gold*, she shared Kay's enthusiasm for asking Cathy to take on the role of Carol. 'When I started work, I felt that the essential thing was to get people from the area – because, although actresses can put on accents, it's a lot harder for them to get the rhythm of the words right,' says Carolyn. 'Cathy was perfect for the part and had acted a lot of northern characters. We wondered whether we should offer her another prostitute role after *Mona Lisa*, but it was a wonderful part and we soon forgot about such con-

Carolyn Bartlett shared Kay Mellor's enthusiasm for asking Cathy Tyson to play Carol

siderations.'

Casting Rose was much more difficult, and the choice of Geraldine James was a surprise to some – including Kay Mellor – but Carolyn had seen her playing a prostitute in the 1970s drama-documentary *Dummy*, and was determined to convince Tony Dennis that she was right for the role. 'Geraldine isn't northern,' says Carolyn, 'but she is a great actress. I thought she was absolutely stunning in *Dummy*, in which she played a deaf and dumb girl. I had been through a list of Yorkshire actresses, but it was tricky to find one in the right age-group. There was only one established actress from Yorkshire that I could find, and, unfortunately, she wasn't available.

'When I first suggested Geraldine to Tony Dennis and the director, Richard Standeven, they looked somewhat surprised – which I suppose is understandable. "She's a middle-class actress," they said. I'm fairly aggressive in my casting and insist that someone should be seen if I feel they're right. And I thought that Geraldine was a really interesting actress, and her beautiful colouring would make a wonderful contrast to Cathy. One of the delights about offering Geraldine the role, too, was that she didn't need to worry about whether it would make or break her career – because it had already been established.'

However, Gina proved to be the most difficult part to cast. Ray Stevenson had already accepted the role of her estranged husband, Steve. 'I saw him playing Macbeth in a Bristol Old Vic Theatre School production,' says Carolyn. 'He was simply sensational. I had 'flu and almost fell out of my seat! And when I found out he was a Geordie, I recommended him to the casting director of *Catherine Cookson's The Dwelling Place*. So, when I was casting for *Band of Gold*, Ray was the only actor that I considered for the part of Steve.'

As a result, Ray was asked to read with the actresses on a shortlist of five who were after the role of Gina, after the dozens initially auditioned had been whittled down. Then Ruth Gemmell was offered the part. 'It was obvious from the moment we saw her that she was the one,' says Tony. 'The magnetism between them was extraordinary, and it came as no surprise that in real life they became an item shortly afterwards.' Carolyn was impressed by Ruth's 'vulnerability, toughness and wonderful self-awareness'.

When Carolyn originally read the scripts she thought that it would be a daunting task to find an actress to play 'sweetie girl' Tracy. 'My heart sank,' she says. 'I wondered how on earth I could get the right person to play a 15-year-old prostitute. Then I received an invitation from the Central Junior Television Workshop, which was holding audi-

'It was obvious from the moment we saw Ruth Gemmell that she was the one to play Gina'

tions at the Groucho Club, in London. Samantha Morton came on and I thought she was sensational. I dragged her into my London office almost immediately. We saw some other actresses, but Sam was the only one we ever seriously considered. I remember sending her to Tony and Richard for the audition: after it, they came down with their eyes out on stalks. She had told them all about her friends and acquaintances in the children's homes she'd been in, and, through that, she already knew quite a bit about the life of prostitutes. When we gave her a camera test, she was just stunning.'

Tony recalls offering Samantha the part of Tracy immediately. 'Sam Morton was a find,' he says. 'She walked in and told us the most amazing story about herself and her life in care in Nottingham – it left us reeling. We had been looking for someone to play her part for a while – but we knew that she was the business. In a rare moment of unanimity, we offered her the job, on the spot. It was the day of her 17th birthday.'

Kay Mellor was also keen for Samantha to play Tracy after she saw her in *Peak Practice*, in which she played a diabetic who was found by a policewoman played by Kay's daughter, Gaynor Faye. 'When Gaynor made that programme,' recalls Kay, 'she returned home and said: "Mum, there's a young girl in *Peak Practice* called Samantha Morton and she's brilliant. She's had an awful life – she was in care from an early age – and I think she could play that part really well." I also saw her shortly afterwards in *Cracker*, in which she played a schoolgirl having an affair with her headmaster. She was someone who was not only young but was a very good actress, and I knew I wanted to do a big story with her.'

The most controversial piece of casting was that of Barbara Dickson – best known as a singer – as madam Anita Braithwaite. Initially, Kay Mellor and Sally Head had their doubts, but Kay admits that Barbara proved to have 'naïve comic potential and delivery'. Again, she got the role because of Carolyn Bartlett's determination and persistence: 'I had seen her back in 1974, in the stage musical *John Paul George Ringo . . . & Bert*, when she was simply sitting there singing and playing the piano,' Carolyn recalls. 'I was there with another Granada casting director, José Scott, and told her that Barbara would make the most wonderful actress. It was just something about her. Then, nine years later, she starred in *Blood Brothers* on stage.

'We had a problem when we came to casting Anita in *Band of Gold*. At the start, we could understand the other parts and the types of actress we wanted to play them, but Anita was very much a cipher. None of us could work her out. I read the script over and over again, but I just couldn't get a grasp of the character. Then, one day, I just said to Tony: "You want someone really different. Why not Barbara Dickson?" He looked astonished and replied: "She's a singer." But I told him: "I bet she can act. She could have been a nightclub singer in a northern town and stayed there."

'Tony and I took Barbara to lunch at the Café Royal and talked about it. As far as I was concerned, she had the role. When we were walking back through Golden Square afterwards, Barbara said to me: "Anita is always one step behind the others, isn't she?" As soon as she said that, I knew the character – she was always running behind the other women, and was always the one who was late. A lot of persuasion was still needed, though, but Tony was happy to go along with the idea when he heard Barbara read for the part. She was the only one who made it to the camera test.'

Portraying reality

Once the lead roles were cast in *Band of Gold*, the actresses and production team were given a chance to research the nature of their characters by meeting Lumb Lane prostitutes at their drop-in centre: the Bradford Working Women's Project.

Cathy Tyson and Geraldine James in costume on Lumb Lane, Bradford, while researching their roles

The women talked about all aspects of their lives, including how much they charged for sex and how they could bring themselves to sleep with men whom they found physically repulsive.

Geraldine James found that her role was to be very different from the prostitute's role that she played in *Dummy*. 'What struck me was that I had played an isolated woman in *Dummy*, but when we researched our roles in *Band of Gold* we were a group of actresses meeting a group of women who weren't so much pals, but, nevertheless, looked out for and understood each other and their differences because they were in competition,' she says. 'We learned a lot from just that one session – not just about the job. For example, we found that they automatically noticed that so-and-so had got into a red Ford at 6.15 and hadn't come back yet. The women had a sharp wit and a way of talking that was terrifying – and very different from mine.'

Cathy Tyson talked to prostitutes in Bradford about their backgrounds, what it was like to be cold outside and how they coped with it. 'I had to acquaint myself with the life before I could act it,' she says. 'I remember a group of lads hit one of them, which was just par for the course, so she had to play it down. That's what struck me. Whenever they get hurt, it's played down. They're the toughest women I have ever met – and they're all individuals. They have to pay the bills and bring up a family. I used to think prostitution was kind of low, but doing the series changed that for me.'

Barbara Dickson found that the experience of meeting the women helped her to understand the environment in which a character such as Anita would exist: 'There were a lot of sensational reports in the press, about these actresses going on the street,' recalls Barbara. 'But we discussed with these women how they felt about their lives and how they dealt with things, and learned a

'Women are interested in the practicalities, such as where prostitutes put the money'

tremendous amount. Women are interested in finding out how such women can do what they do for a living and conduct a normal life as well. Women are interested in the practicalities: such as where prostitutes put the money – in their shoes, is often the answer – and when is a good time for business.'

Richard Standeven, who was to direct the first two episodes of *Band of Gold*, production designer Chris Wilkinson, costume designer Sue Peck and make-up designer Sue Milton all gained valuable insights into the prostitutes' world on this visit to Bradford. The actresses were also dressed in their prostitute gear and sent on the streets to see whether they would attract potential clients. 'Everyone concerned with the programme was determined that the world it portrayed should be as authentic and credible as we could make it,' says producer, Tony Dennis. 'Richard carried out extensive research in Bradford and Manchester. Richard Laxton and Charles Beeson, who directed the other episodes, were also keen to make sure that everything was authentic. In part, this was because, like almost everyone else on the programme, they had no real experience of the lives that these women lived or the communities that they came from.'

Locations

The task of finding appropriate sets and locations for *Band of Gold* fell to production designer Chris Wilkinson. Filming was to take place on the real Lumb Lane, in Bradford, and in and around Manchester, where Granada Television is based. 'The story was set in Yorkshire,' says Chris, 'and it's a pretty seedy part of Yorkshire at that. We took quite a few trips round Lumb Lane and the Manningham red-light area of Bradford, and spoke to prostitutes there. But that wasn't so much to give me ideas for sets as to get a feel for the whole production – it gave me my first insight into what life there was like.

'We planned to film in Lumb Lane, but we were limited as to what we could do there. One of the key locations was the school attended by Carol's daughter, Emma – and the one we used was good, because you could see the hills surrounding Bradford in the distance. But the only interiors filmed in Bradford were at the Town Hall. We didn't think that it warranted filming all the street scenes in the city because that would require taking a unit from Manchester to Bradford and putting everyone up in a hotel, which is expensive.

'So we looked for something in or near Manchester that would match Lumb Lane, which is a predominantly Asian area. It was a problem because the buildings in Manchester are generally constructed with red bricks, whereas in Yorkshire stone is used in the main. So we tried to pick as many rendered buildings as possible or others that weren't obviously red-brick. Eventually, I found somewhere in Ashton-under-Lyne that had a similar feel to that of the Manningham district of Bradford. It's part of Stamford Street, which was the main street running through the town until the bypass was built. I gave one end of it, which is now quiet and partly disused, an Asian flavour by creating tandoori restaurants, printing works and Asian factories, mainly by adding frontages to the buildings. Some shops and pubs were still in business: so a wedding-gown shop was transformed into a sari shop; an alternative medicine shop became a tandoori restaurant; a video store was turned into an Asian video store; and two pubs were given different names – the Red Lion became the Hustler's Arms, where the prostitutes met. The interior of the Red Lion was similar to those of the pubs on Lumb Lane, so I had very little work to do – apart from substituting Yorkshire Breweries signs for Boddington's Bitter ones, taking down the Lowry prints and painting the inside darker.'

'I gave her a 1940s cocktail bar and 1950s furniture, and the wallpaper was very floral and over-the-top'

An empty apartment over an existing tandoori restaurant in nearby Old Street was turned into Anita's flat. Doing this was much better than building a studio set, because you could see industrial land and high-rise flats from the window. 'I made Anita's flat a bit kitsch after talking to the costume designer about how she was going to dress her,' recalls Chris. 'She was into leotards, leopard-skins and tight trousers. When the character is more upfront, as Anita was, it gives you more of a clue about what you can do with the set. I gave her a 1940s cocktail bar and 1950s furniture. The wallpaper was very floral and over-the-top, and the back room of the flat was decorated as Anita's spare room, which she rented out to the prostitutes. That's where Gina had sex for the first time after going on the game. When we needed to show Anita's bedroom, I just redecorated the same room.'

The exterior for Carol's house was found in Salford. 'It was a council house-type in quite a tidy cul-de-sac where filming could be easily controlled,' says Chris. 'It was also a house that you wouldn't expect a prostitute to work from, because Carol had two sides to her: the family side, which made her very protective of her daughter Emma, and the prostitute side. The interior of Carol's house was built as two composite sets – downstairs and upstairs – at Spectrum Arena, a former sports hall at Birchwood, near Warrington. Kay Mellor wanted me to paint all of the interior white because Carol was obsessed with cleanliness. It was a good idea, but white tends to be a bit too strong for television. We compromised, and I painted it in light colours. A pink sofa is delivered in one of the early scenes, which helped to emphasize Carol's domesticity.'

Chris found a house in Manningham that could be used when filming the exterior of Gina's house. The interior was built as ground-floor and first-floor composite sets at Spectrum Arena. But, because she had three children, the house was made to look more run-down and lived-in than Carol's. 'She was a modern woman in her early twenties,' says Chris. 'So I went round B&Q and looked at the wallpaper, light-fittings and other kinds of decoration that people of her age were buying, because stores like that are always full of young mums. I came up with inexpensive decor for her house: striped green below the dado; a floral dado; and a green floral pattern above it.

'The exterior of the house of Gina's mother, Joyce, was in Stalybridge, on the outskirts of Manchester – on the way towards Yorkshire – it's quite hilly and the buildings are constructed from rendered stone. It was in a cul-de-sac of small, grey stucco terraced houses – ideal for Joyce and her boyfriend Bob. Gina would have been brought up here, and there's a much older feeling to this house than to her own. Again, the interior of Joyce's house was built at Spectrum, but it was just a ground-floor composite this time – along with a separate bedroom set for the scene in which Joyce finds Bob's scrapbooks of newspaper cuttings about Gina's murder.'

The scene of Gina's murder, in the first episode, was filmed on wasteland in Broughton, on the outskirts of Manchester, and the leisure centre and swimming pool scenes featured in the last episode of the first series were shot in Bolton. The film crew travelled to a house in Harrogate for interior and exterior scenes of Tracy's parents' house, and Chris used Davyhulme Park Hospital, which is on the outskirts of Manchester, for Tracy's hospital scenes.

Rose's Bradford flat was only seen briefly in the series. Chris found a suitable ground-floor flat in Ashton-under-Lyne that belonged to an Asian, and which had very colourful interior decor. He

'I had to soundproof the windows because the noise from the trains was horrendous'

turned it into the type of home in which Rose would live by opting for 'extremely dowdy' wall paper, of the kind Rose would choose.

Although there was some location filming in London, for the part of the story in which Rose and Tracy lived in the capital, the scenes set in their London flat were shot in Manchester. 'One of the main criteria was that the director wanted to overlook a railway line, supposedly running into King's Cross,' says Chris. 'So we followed the line out of Manchester, getting on a train at Piccadilly station and taking a trip towards Stockport. We ended up finding somewhere back in Manchester, over a pub next to Piccadilly station!

'I had to soundproof the windows because the noise from the trains was horrendous. The flat gave us a big living area, which we needed because Tracy was still doing tricks and bringing punters back home. We wanted a large, interesting room that wasn't obviously in Manchester: this one had quite nice architectural detail, with a big fireplace and a large mirror above it, and was very sparsely furnished. We kept Rose's bedroom very much as it was, but we painted the big bedroom that Tracy used red and deliberately made it more tarty. Tracy was heavily into drugs at that time, and everything she did was chilled out, so it seemed appropriate to have candles and silks over all the light fittings.'

The night scenes set in London's Soho were filmed there, but day scenes were shot in Tib Street, in the centre of Manchester. The Blue Gardenia, which Tracy frequented in the London scenes, was actually the 42nd Street club in Manchester: 'That's a big club, so I put in a lot of different light fittings, made it quite gloomy and gave it a seedy feel,' says Chris. 'I also built a huge circular mirror for a stunt in which Tracy goes on to the stage area and throws a bar stool through the mirror.'

INNOCENT
UNTIL
PROVED
GUILTY.

3

Band of Gold 1

Filming for the first series began in the late summer of 1994. Richard Standeven, who directed the first two episodes and had the job of setting a style for the series, was clear about the result he was looking for on screen: 'It was a rough series,' he recalls, 'and I didn't want the style of camerawork to be glossy, still or conventional. So the scene in which Gina screams when she finds a debt collector taking her possessions away was filmed with a hand-held camera, which gave it a semi-documentary feel. The other factor that helped to get the look right was the locations, which were a little bare.

'Throughout filming, I pushed all the actors really hard,' says Richard. 'On the first day, Ruth Gemmell, who played Gina, went home crying because I asked so much of her in terms of portraying emotions and the way she delivered certain lines. Gina was such an important character that I

The hierarchy of Lumb Lane is evident in the first meeting of Rose (Geraldine James) and Gina (Ruth Gemmell)

A CERTAIN CHEMISTRY: RAY STEVENSON AND RUTH GEMMELL

Playing the grieving husband of prostitute Gina Dixon led actor Ray Stevenson to fall for his murdered screen wife away from the cameras. As Steve Dixon, Ray portrayed a violent husband whose wife had thrown him out after he hit her. She was so desperate for money to feed herself and her three children that she went on the game, and was murdered.

Geordie Ray only appeared alongside actress Ruth Gemmell, who played Gina, in one episode, but they hit it off immediately and now live together. Ruth was one of five actresses with whom Ray read lines during auditions for the role of Gina, and the chemistry between them was obvious to all those present. Ruth's character was killed at the end of the first episode, but Ray went on to appear in the first two series of *Band of Gold*, which gave him plenty of opportunity to develop the character of Steve.

'I wanted to make him real,' says Ray. 'He wasn't a sinner – he was just an ordinary bloke from the north. The great thing about Kay Mellor's writing is that none of her characters are all bad and none are all good: she carefuly avoids the stereotypes. Just when you've made judgements about people, she goes and proves you wrong.

'When you first meet Steve, Gina has thrown him out after he lashed out at her, and he has been unemployed for two years. So he's at a particularly low ebb. By the end of the first series, he's trying to come to terms with Gina's death. All along, he has been looking for a job.'

After his moving portrayal of Steve in *Band of Gold*, Ray starred in Kay Mellor's television film, *Some Kind of Life*, as a man severely injured in a motorcycle accident. Ray and Ruth Gemmell also played a husband and wife in an episode of *Peak Practice*. 'They went for the package,' says Ray, who is the only actor to have appeared in two Catherine Cookson adaptations: *The Dwelling Place* and *The Tide of Life*. He also teamed up with Geraldine James again in the BBC series *Drovers' Gold*, playing a Geordie called Armstrong.

had to concentrate a lot on Ruth. But my biggest problem was not to let the performances get too big. It was the north of England, and everyone was wearing distinctive clothes, so suddenly I would find them all over-acting like mad. We had, however, largely overcome this by the time rehearsals had finished.'

From the start, writer Kay Mellor kept a close eye on her baby to ensure that her vision reached the screen intact. One early scene was even re-filmed after Kay saw the 'rushes' – the daily reels of film shot – and discovered that the character of Carol Johnson had been given the stereotypical image of a prostitute: 'When you are first introduced to Carol in the programme, she's coming downstairs,' says Kay. 'I wanted her to be wearing a T-shirt and jeans. But when I saw the rushes, she was wearing a red satin bra and knickers. I said: "I don't want that." They *did* reshoot it for me: she came down wearing a white towelling dressing-gown. I was really pleased that they did that. It's really important how the characters are first viewed. Now Carol's wearing a white dressing-gown when you first meet her – she's a mother, she's clean and she has a nice house. Similarly, Gina is portrayed as a housewife.'

Two violent scenes with Gina's widowed husband, Steve, were co-ordinated by stunt arranger Stuart St Paul. He describes them as 'a couple of edgy fights', pointing out that he wanted to put across the characters involved rather than the violence itself. In the first scene, Steve has sex with Carol after finding out that his wife had teamed up with Carol before her murder. After getting out of bed, Steve confronts her. 'Violence against women is a very dodgy subject to deal with on television,' says Stuart, 'and it's very difficult to make squabbles between men and women look real without actually putting the violence on screen. Rather than him slapping her around, I had the vision of Steve screaming and the aggression building up to the point where he stuffs the money in Carol's mouth.'

As a result of this incident, DCI Newall – who was investigating Gina's murder and had previously been transferred away from the vice squad because of his relationship with Carol – speeds off in his car to see Steve. The result is another struggle, which also had to be choreographed by Stuart: 'We had a situation in which two guys were angry with each other,' he says. 'I didn't want them to get into a fist fight in a living room, so I put the sofa in between them, making the fight a squabble across the furniture, which makes things more interesting.'

Gina was filmed on the streets in 'bare' locations to give a semi-documentary feel to the programme

By the time of the second murder of a prostitute – Carol look-alike Amanda Smeaton – a whodunit scenario was developing. Half-a-dozen suspects emerged, and viewers had to wait until the final episode to discover the killer's true identity. Newspapers joined in, presenting readers with the clues – including the fact that the killer drove a red Vauxhall Cavalier – and asked celebrities to guess the murderer's identity.

Kay Mellor kept a close eye on her baby to ensure that her vision reached the screen intact

When Rose finally decided to break out of prostitution, she left for London and Tracy went with her. Rose was encouraged to take a business course by Richard, who was in charge of a drop-in centre, and the pair had a relationship. This enabled writer Kay Mellor to explore what it is like for prostitutes to fall in love. The scenes were not included in the original scripts written for the BBC, because only

Stunt arranger Stuart St Paul set up the scene where Gina's widowed husband, Steve, stuffs cash into Carol's mouth after having sex, and confronts her about his wife's decision to go on the game

four episodes had been commissioned then, rather than the six that were made by Granada. 'A lot of prostitutes know about acting sex,' explains Kay, 'but few know very much about their own sexuality. Their job is to satisfy men: you may think that they are highly sophisticated sexual beings, but they're not like that at all.'

Stunt arranger Stuart St Paul was on hand to ensure that everything went according to plan when Tracy was seen high on drugs, throwing a bar stool at a mirror in the Blue Gardenia nightclub – in reality, the 42nd Street Club, in Manchester: 'It had to be done in one take,' he recalls, 'so, rather than have an actress throw the stool, miss and break the set – which would then need to be rebuilt – I threw the stool at the mirror myself.'

Throughout the filming, producer Tony Dennis felt that it was important to portray the grim realities of prostitutes' lives in a northern city: 'I was deeply concerned that it should be done

properly,' he says. 'In the end, what we delivered was certainly darker and bleaker than some people might have expected. Michael Wearing, who ultimately took the decision to pass on the project at the BBC, told me that the series would have been entirely different if it had been made for them. His implication was that it would have been sanitized: made softer, and more frilly. It would have been easy for the programme to go that way. After all, the main characters were hookers selling sex, which sells just about everything in our consumerist culture. I thought it was crucial that we got a sense of their world, and the dismal and relentless pressure that kept these women out on street corners, offering their bodies for sale in the wet and cold: There was a tension in Kay's writing that could be simultaneously gritty and realistic, on the one hand, and delightfully funny, on the other – while servicing authentic characters. But, in some other areas, the narrative was

Playing tragic roles has become something of a career stock-in-trade for actress Rachel Davies, who was especially moving as shop steward Pauline, who was stricken by cancer, in the comedy-drama series *Making Out;* and, just before joining *Band of Gold*, she played Alan Turner's short-lived wife, Shirley, in *Emmerdale*: her character was shot dead in the bloody aftermath of a post office raid. A former prostitute, Shirley had given up the game to start afresh, working in the soup kitchen of a drop-in centre.

It was *Band of Gold* casting director Carolyn Bartlett's good fortune that she happened to be speaking to Rachel's agent when she was looking for an actress to play Gina Dixon's distraught mother, Joyce Webster: 'I had thought Rachel was in *Emmerdale*,' says Carolyn. 'But Rachel's agent said: "what about Rachel?" and told me that her part in the programme had finished two weeks earlier.'

Rachel was auditioned and the role of Joyce was hers, though the death of her screen daughter in the first episode meant that the actress was seen in tears or suppressed anger for most of the series. Joyce also felt extremely guilty because she had refused to look after her three grandchildren when Gina wanted to get a job Instead, Gina became a prostitute and was murdered by a punter. Consequently, Kay Mellor was able to focus more on Joyce's grief after Granada Television commissioned her to expand the original four episodes to make a six-part series.

Manchester-born Rachel, who was brought up in Blackpool, appeared on stage with Laurence Olivier in Eugene O'Neill's *Long Day's Journey Into Night* at the National Theatre. She acted in *Coronation Street* in the 1970s, playing Post Office canteen worker Donna Parker, to whom Alf Roberts loaned £500. She later played secretary Elaine Winters in *Crossroads* and divorcée Doreen Evans in *Boon* — she helped out at the Grand Hotel and fell for Ken Boon, played by Michael Elphick. She has also played parts in *Heartbeat* and *Cracker*. Rachel has also appeared in the films *Yanks*, *A Private Function* and *Knights and Emeralds*.

underpowered. The view of the world and the thriller dimension were aspects that we worked at together, to anchor the story and drive it on.'

Tony is full of praise for those who worked behind the scenes on that first series of *Band of Gold*. 'Costume designer Sue Peck, make-up designer Sue Milton, production designer Chris Wilkinson, director of photography Peter Jessop and their teams astonished everybody by the extent of their labours and by their enthusiasm for the programme,' he says. 'Peter and camera operator Michael McCleery helped to achieve that

RUTH GEMMELL
AS GINA

The tragic story of young mother Gina Dixon, murdered after going on the game to pay off her debts, brought the dangers of prostitution home to actress Ruth Gemmell. 'It's the oldest profession,' says Ruth 'and won't just go away. It's daft just to clear it off the streets, because it's going to happen somewhere else. It needs to be legalized, so that it can be controlled. Kerb-crawling shouldn't happen any more. Within a controlled environment, the dangers can be limited.

'Before filming we went to Bradford and were introduced to some of the girls working the Lane. They were fascinating to listen to; they're a lot more vulnerable than they admit, but they are also a lot more human than you might think – they're very normal. I didn't ask that many questions, because my character was going into it with her head in the sand, which was why she ended up dead.

'Gina had three children and a broken marriage. Her husband, Steve, wasn't much help with the children and any work she found wasn't enough. She met Carol Johnson as they picked their children up from school. Carol had her life under control and had money to spare. Because prostitution appeared to be a means to an end, Gina modelled herself on Carol. She had a cosmetics round and left home in the evenings under the guise of being the Aveyron lady!'

Gina teamed up with Carol, and, while Gina had sex with one of her first clients, Carol robbed him of £50. Later, Gina made the mistake of going out on the streets on her own, and was picked up by the client, Ian, who drove her to the moors, where he murdered her. Ian later killed a black prostitute, believing her to be Carol.

'Gina was wonderful to play,' recalls Ruth, who was seen only in the first episode. 'Throughout the first series, no one forgot Gina. If the public remember me for anything, it is for that role. Many people wrote to me saying they had enjoyed the programme.'

Ruth subsequently played moody Detective Con Kerry in the BBC series *Silent Witness*, starring Amanda Burton as a pathologist. This time her character survived for more than one episode but she was accidentally killed at the end of the series, when a pipe fell on her head during a police search of a hospital boiler room.

Further recognition came for Ruth when she starred with Colin Firth in the 1997 feature film *Fever Pitch*, a romantic comedy adapted by Nick Hornby from his best-selling autobiographical novel about a teacher obsessed with Arsenal Football Club. Ruth played his girlfriend, Sarah, who had to compete with Arsenal for his affections: 'It's the biggest thing I've done professionally since *Band of Gold*,' she says. 'The film had a lot of publicity when it opened and I hope something good comes out of that for me.'

Working on *Fever Pitch* with the heart-throb who played Darcy in *Pride and Prejudice* on television was an honour for Ruth, but she only had eyes for her off-screen partner, actor Ray Stevenson, who played her violent estranged husband, Steve, in *Band of Gold*. The couple first met while making the programme and now live together in London. 'We have no plans to marry,' says Ruth, 'but maybe one day.'

Ruth, born in Bristol but brought up in County Durham, always wanted to act. She was fortunate enough to find stage work immediately after attending drama school in London. On stage, she has played Desdemona in *Othello*, Isabella in *Measure for Measure*, Yelena in *Uncle Vanya* and Perdita in *The Winter's Tale*. Since making her television debut as a staff nurse in the mini-series *You Me and It*, Ruth has appeared on the small screen in *In Suspicious Circumstances*, *The Bill*, *Kavanagh QC*, an episode of *Peak Practice* with Ray Stevenson, again playing husband and wife, and the one-off romantic comedy *The Perfect Blue*, playing an air hostess obsessed with tidiness.

Tony Doyle, who had just played Chief Superintendent John Deakin in three series of *Between the Lines*, found himself on the wrong side of the law when he joined *Band of Gold* as George Ferguson, who owned a cleaning business and provided his mistress, Anita, with a flat. He has since become even better known as loveable rogue Brian Quigley in *Ballykissangel*.

David Schofield was cast as DCI Newall, the policeman leading the hunt for Gina Dixon's murderer. David is known for playing baddies on TV, in programmes such as *Van Der Valk*, *Bergerac*, *Taggart* and *The Bill*, but his first acting break came as the hideously deformed John Merrick in the original stage play of *The Elephant Man*.

Richard Moore played Curly, the weird-looking punter who paid Carol to 'walk' for him in black five-denier stockings while he wore rubber gloves. Richard was born in Burnley, but now lives with his wife and two children in a picturesque Cornish village. He previously played Audrey Roberts's boyfriend George Hepworth in *Coronation Street*, before she married Alf.

Richard Hope starred in the series *The Riff Raff Element* and *Tears Before Bedtime* before joining *Band of Gold* as Richard, Rose's do-gooding lover in London. Before becoming an actor, Richard gained a degree in law.

Barbara Marten, who made her television debut in *Coronation Street* as Alma Baldwin's friend Doreen Braithwaite, took the role of Tracy's mother, Helen Richards. Barbara also played Sheila Grant's sister in *Brookside* and has had gritty roles in *The Fifteen Streets* and *Harry*.

John Bowler, previously best known as David Lynch in the sitcom *Watching*, played Tracy's father, Tim Richards. He has since had roles in series such as Catherine Cookson's *The Tide of Life* and *The Sculptress* and the 'Screen Two' drama *Stone Scissors Paper*.

grungy, feel-of-the-street ambience that served the series so well, I think.'

The producer was also pleased with the on-screen partnership struck up between Geraldine James and Samantha Morton. 'Geraldine is a consummate professional,' he says. 'She was brilliant, both in her creation of Rose and in the outstanding support she offered Sam. They really were impressive together, and Geraldine's selflessness was humbling.' Tony also recalls the humour that crept into working conditions that were sometimes difficult: 'Barbara Dickson was delightful as Anita and really got her teeth into the part,' he says. 'She provided me with one of the best moments of the shoot. When Director Richard Laxton asked for yet another take, at 3.30 in the morning on a cold, wet Ashton-under-Lyne street, Barbara's scripted line to Geraldine James – "You can stick it up your arse," – seemed positively inspired!'

First reactions

When the first two episodes of *Band of Gold* were shown to the press, a few weeks before transmission, it was an anxious time for the programme's creator, producer and cast. Kay Mellor travelled to London for the screening with Trea, the real-life prostitute on whom Carol's character was based. This was the moment of truth for Kay, as she sat with the woman whose story was unfolding on screen: 'I was so nervous,' she remembers. 'At the end, I turned to look at Trea and tears were pouring down her face. I asked her if it was all right and she said: "Yes, you wrote it like it is." I was so choked. I didn't give a damn at that moment what the press thought. I would have felt that I had failed if she hadn't liked it. My whole reason for writing it was to give prostitutes a voice – I was euphoric after that.'

The press also gave *Band of Gold* an ecstatic reception: many journalists sat though the screening open-mouthed and stunned. 'They probably didn't know what to think, or how the general public would receive it,' says Kay. 'They had nothing to gauge it by. I think they felt that viewers would either love it or loathe it – there would be no middle ground. So they had to make up their own minds.'

The first episode of *Band of Gold* was screened on Sunday 12 March 1995. The series became an instant hit, regularly attracting more than 15 million viewers and became the only programme to challenge *Coronation Street* in the ratings: 'It did absolutely brilliantly,' says Sally Head, who, as Granada's controller of drama, was executive producer of the first series. 'On the day the first episode was broadcast, I remember Tony Dennis telling us that his wife, a doctor, had prayed that it would get 15 million viewers and we roared with laughter. 'But, the next day, to our amazement, we heard that the overnight viewing figures gave us 11.5 million. It was way beyond what we expected. Two days later, everyone – writer, actors and producer – all came to my office for gallons of champagne to celebrate. We were just so overwhelmed.

'During the party, I was called away to answer a telephone call. I was told that the overnight viewing figures had been messed up during that week, and that they could be wrong by at least two or three million. I asked, "Do you mean up or down?" The man on the other end of the telephone said, "Down." I just couldn't go back into my office and tell anyone, so at the time I just kept quiet about it. In fact, we found out later that we had lost a million – but then the figure built up to 15 million and there was no doubt – our prayer had been answered after all.'

In the event, *Band of Gold* became Granada Television's most popular drama series ever, attracting more viewers than classics such as *Brideshead Revisited*, *The Jewel in the Crown*, *Prime Suspect* and *Cracker*, and winning almost 60 per cent of the television audience – almost double the number that watched BBC1's adaptation of Joanna Trollope's *The Choir*, which ran at the same time. *Band of Gold* was sold to more than a dozen countries, including America, Australia, Thailand, Croatia and Sweden, and won the Birmingham Film and Television Festival Samuelson Award for Television, and the American CableACE Award for Best Drama. Make-up designer Sue Milton, praised by Tony Dennis for her 'perceptiveness and diligence', won the Royal Television Society Craft and Design Award for Best Make-up.

'Tears were pouring down Trea's face. I asked her if it was all right and she said: " Yes, you wrote it like it is."'

BAND OF GOLD 1: THE STORY

Episode One: Sold

Twenty-three-year-old Gina Dixon, a mother-of-three who has left her violent husband, Steve, and sells make-up door-to-door to earn money, turns to prostitution in an attempt to pay off her debt. She teams up with hooker Carol Johnson and is murdered after getting into a car and being driven to the moors.

Gina Dixon tells her mother, Joyce Webster, that she needs a full-time job. But Joyce says that she cannot look after her daughter's children, Joanne, Sarah and Michelle. 'I don't want lumbering wi' kids now, not at my age,' she says. When Gina returns home, she is confronted by debt collector Mr Moore: 'You owe me two months' money – I want £180,' he shouts. She tells him she has nothing and he leaves, saying he will return on Friday. If she does not have the money, he will take her belongings.

On Friday morning, desperate for money, Gina sets off to see estranged husband Steve in a house in Bradford. Unwilling to tell him of her real predicament, she asks him for cash to buy new shoes for Sarah. When Steve says he has nothing, Gina leaves, threatening to divorce him.

Gina, who is separated from her husband and desperate for money to pay off her debts, tells Carol that she needs to earn some 'proper money' and goes on the game

Gina Dixon left husband Steve after he broke her tooth and now has to bring up three children by herself. Aged 23, she has a make-up round to make ends meet, but her desperation to pay off a debt collector leads her to go on the game. At first she teams up with Carol Johnson, but she meets a violent end when she goes her own way.

Rose Garrity is past her sell-by date but still doing business. At 38, she rules the Lane with a rod of iron and is jealous of the younger women. She has a hard exterior – she smokes and swears – but a soft centre, and is desperate to give up life on the game. After trying to drum schoolgirl hooker Tracy Richards out of the Lane, she takes the teenager under her wing.

Carol Johnson is the daughter of a prostitute, and became one herself at the age of 13. She is a single mother to daughter Emma. She walks the Lane and is desperate to earn enough money to get off the streets. She finds herself in demand with an apparent weirdo called Curly, then becomes paranoid and obsessed with cleaning after a murderer takes the lives of two prostitutes. Finally, she cracks.

Anita Braithwaite is in love with married businessman and loan shark George Ferguson, who provides her with a flat. A former croupier, she is nice but dim. She does, however, charge her friends on the game to use her spare bedroom for business. Panic sets in when she is left with a vanity case belonging to murdered prostitute Gina Dixon.

Tracy Richards is the daughter of middle-class parents and a victim of her father's sexual abuse. Her real name is Naomi. Tracy ran away from home and went on the game at 15 and now lives in fear of her violent pimp, Dez Sadiq, who has hooked her on drugs. At first she is resented by ageing hooker Rose Garrity, who rules the Lane, but they become closer when the street girls close ranks after Gina's murder.

Joyce Webster is the divorced mother of murdered prostitute Gina Dixon. She is distraught when she hears of her daughter's murder and to discover that she was on the game. She works as a cleaner for George Ferguson's business, Klenzit UK, lives with a lover called Bob and has to care for Gina's three children.

She arrives home to find Moore and a heavy removing a television and video recorder from the house. She becomes hysterical, and Moore refrains from taking the microwave oven and leaves, adding, however, that he will be back at the end of the month.

The following day, Gina visits prostitute Carol Johnson, whose daughter, Emma, goes to the same

Feeling threatened by the prostitutes on the Lane after Rose warned a punter away from 'sweetie girl'
Tracy, her pimp, Dez, tells Carol to leave Tracy alone and steals her money

school as Gina's daughter, Joanne, and says she is no longer selling make-up for Aveyron. Gina tells Carol that she needs to earn 'some proper money' So, after Carol has shown a regular client out of the house, she shows Gina her bedroom, with hand-cuffs hanging from the headboard, and gets into the bath, scrubbing herself with a nailbrush. Gina then listens as Carol tells her about what she does and how much money she earns – she suggests that she could do the same, but Carol tries to dissuade her from doing so.

When Carol takes Gina to the Hustler's Arms, Gina is approached by older prostitute Rose Garrity, who asks what she is doing. 'This is my patch,' says Rose. 'She wants to work the Lane,' Carol says. Rose retorts: 'You wanna work the Lane, you ask me.' 'I'm asking,' says Gina.

> *'You wanna work the Lane, you ask me.'*
> *'I'm asking,' says Gina*

Anita Braithwaite, whose married lover George Ferguson provides her with a flat, is a madam who rents out a bedroom for Gina to use with clients, at £2 for half-an-hour. Her first client, arranged by Carol, is called Ashley. He believes that she is 17 and a virgin. When they have finished, Gina washes her face and sets off home, where she finds that her mother has left the children with Steve, who gives her £30 that he has borrowed from a friend. Hoping for a reconciliation, he promises not to hit Gina again, but after she points out that he said that the previous time, he leaves. So Gina goes to the Lane with Carol and waits for business. An attractive woman pulls up in her car and asks how much they charge. Gina, who is still naïve does not understand, but Carol eagerly steps in saying '£50 – for both of us'.

Several days later, a client called Ian – who is 'in security' – takes Gina to his large Victorian house. While they are in the bedroom, Carol snoops around the front room. Ian asks to see Gina again, but she refuses and sets off with Carol. As they leave Carol tells Gina to run.

At the Hustler's Arms, Carol hands £50 to Gina, which she stole from the house, but Gina is annoyed that her friend should steal from a client. In the pub's toilets Gina counts £145 in her handbag and scribbles the figure on the back of Carol's Avcyron order form, subtracts it from the £180 that she still owes and sees that she has only to earn £35 more.

That evening Rose sees 15-year-old prostitute Tracy Richards on the Lane chatting up a punter through the window of his van. Rose frightens the potential client away by shouting that the police are after Tracy. 'Go play with yer Wendy house,' Rose shouts at her. Later, Tracy hands the money she has earned during the day over to her pimp, Dez Sadiq, and explains what happened.

Meanwhile, in the Hustler's Arms, a middle-aged, curly-haired man hands Carol three £10 notes and asks where her friend is. Meanwhile, Gina arrives at Anita's flat and asks her to look after her vanity case. Anita is nervous because it is Thursday, when George visits. Taking the case and getting rid of Gina, Anita closes the door to be confronted by George, who says, 'I'd better go.' As he leaves, Anita retorts: 'Screw me and sod off, that's all you ever do.'

As Gina stands in a dark stretch of the Lane waiting for business, a car stops a little way behind her, with its headlights on full beam. She shields her eyes from the glare. The passenger door is flung open, she gets in and is driven to a piece of wasteland. 'Why've we come here?' asks Gina. 'Where are we going?' The man stops the car, puts a cassette of *Gymnopedie No. 1* by Erik Satie into the tape deck and plays it. Gina tries to open the door, and, discovering that it is locked, she becomes hysterical.

Meanwhile, in the Lane, Tracy's pimp, Dez, drives up to Carol. When she sees it is him, Carol runs off, but he chases her, grabs her and takes her into a derelict building. Putting a knife to Carol's throat, Dez tells her to leave Tracy alone; then he steals her money.

Back on the wasteland, a man walking his two dogs finds Gina's bloodied body – she is dead. DC Jameson arrives on the scene, finds money in her handbag and says: 'She wasn't murdered for money, then.' DCI Newall looks inside the bag and finds the Averyon order form with the figures

'What am I going to do with this?' asks Anita, holding Gina's vanity case after her murder

written on it and Carol's name and address on the other side. The police tell Carol and Rose that Gina has been murdered. In a state of shock, they rush to tell Anita. 'Stupid bitch must have been workin' by herself,' says Carol. Anita, who still has Gina's vanity case, takes it out of a cupboard and asks, 'What am I going to do with this?' Rose chips in: 'The only way we're gonna sort this out is if we all stick together.'

Episode Two: Caught

The prostitutes on the Lane close ranks after the murder of Gina, with Rose and Carol trying to persuade 'sweetie girl' Tracy to work with them – to the annoyance of her pimp, Dez. Weird-looking Curly pays Carol to 'walk' for him in a hotel, and she tries to ensure her safety by taking Rose and Tracy along. Later, Tracy is hit over the head and left for dead.

On the day after the murder, DCI Newall visits Carol and shows her a photograph of Gina and then the cosmetics order form. She tells the detective that Gina was selling make-up to pay off a loan. Meanwhile, news reporters gather outside Gina's house and a distraught Joyce Webster visits her boss, George Ferguson, in his office at the cleaning business. She breaks down as she tells him that she has to take time off to look after her grandchildren.

Rose and Carol take teenage prostitute Tracy under their wing as the women on the streets start to fear for their lives. Tracy is shocked to learn that Gina had only been on the game for a week. Anita offers Tracy the use of her flat at £2.50 per half-hour – a 50p increase on her previous rate. The weird-looking man who had previously asked Carol about Gina enters the pub, sits down with a drink and smiles at the women. As Carol approaches him and starts talking, Tracy's pimp, Dez, arrives and tells her to leave with him. As he waits outside, Tracy tells Rose and Anita, 'He'll kill me now.' Meanwhile, Curly – who is talking to Carol – pulls the sleeve of

his jacket over a scab on the back of his left hand, which arouses Carol's suspicions. Then he offers £100 to see her again.

Outside, in Dez's car, the pimp hits Tracy across the face as he tells her to stay away from the other prostitutes; then he hands her 'a little lifter' – some speed. Confused, she gets out of the car and Rose and Carol walk out of the pub as he roars off. They split up and Rose bumps into Tracy: 'What do you think you're doin'?' she asks. 'Waiting for you,' Tracy replies.

As Carol turns into the alley near her house, she is confronted by Curly. He offers her £150, which she refuses. He increases the amount to £200, and she agrees to meet him in a hotel room. Rose warns her of the dangers, but Carol insists that she cannot come to any harm, pointing out that Gina was found on the moor.

As Joyce tells her father about Gina's death, Carol opens her door to Councillor Baker, who is there on the pretence that he is doing research about the new leisure centre. Once inside, she shows him upstairs and, with an apron tied round her waist, spanks him with a wooden spoon.

At Gina's funeral, Joyce is consumed with guilt, recalling her refusal to look after her daughter's children. DCI Newall looks on and wonders whether Gina's husband, Steve, could be the murderer. Later, Newall and Steve make a television appeal for any information about Gina's black vanity case. Anita subsequently goes to Turton Lane police station and tells Newall: 'I was just minding it for a friend of a friend.'

At the Norfolk Gardens Hotel, Carol, Rose and Tracy are let in a back entrance by a willing male employee called Tommy: it is the venue for Carol's meeting with Curly, and Rose and Tracy are there to protect her. When Curly arrives, he goes up to Room 315, on the third floor, with Carol. At the same time, Rose is being chatted up at the hotel bar by a salesman. Carol phones her baby-sitter to make sure that her daughter is all right and has a short chat with Emma.

Carol and Curly climb the stairs to the third floor of the hotel – she is insistent that she will not go in the lift – while Rose and Tracy are stopped by the hotel manager, who knows that they are prostitutes and tells them they must leave. As Carol starts to undress, Curly tells her to keep her clothes on. He takes a pair of rubber gloves from his briefcase, puts them on and holds a pair of black nylon stockings. Curly appears to be turning aggressive, telling Carol: 'I could hurt you.' Convinced that she is about to be murdered, Carol starts screaming.

Rose and Tracy beg the manager not to throw

Joyce is consumed with guilt, recalling her refusal to look after her daughter's children

them out of the hotel, saying that Carol's life is in danger. The three of them rush to Room 315 and bang on the door. But, to Rose and Tracy's surprise, Carol calmly opens the door, dressed in black stockings and high-heeled shoes. Curly, who is sitting on a sofa at the far side of the room, wearing a pair of pink rubber gloves, explains that everything is in order. The manager escorts Rose away while Tommy goes into the room next door, where Tracy is waiting for him.

'You'll have to start again – only this time do it slower,' Curly tells Carol. She goes into the bathroom and, as he has asked, explains in detail how

At Gina's funeral, mother Joyce and husband Steve confront their guilt: she over her refusal to look after the grandchildren so that Gina could take a job; he over the violence that led to their marital split

GERALDINE JAMES AS ROSE

Playing ageing hooker Rose Garrity in *Band of Gold* brought actress Geraldine James full circle. She first won television acclaim at 27, as deaf and dumb Sandra, rejected by society and forced into backstreet prostitution, in the dramatized documentary *Dummy* in 1977. At the age of 44 she was acting a prostitute again, although Rose was only 38.

'I'm a middle-class girl from Maidenhead, and the only way that I could have played Rose in *Band of Gold* was through having acted a prostitute in *Dummy*,' says Geraldine. 'Sandra was an extraordinary part to play – a trillion miles away from me. Franc Roddam, the director, was so fed up with trying to find someone to play the part that he took the evening off to watch television. As a result, he saw me in my first TV role, as Dennis Waterman's girlfriend in an episode of *The Sweeney*, and thought I had a quality similar to the character, but difficult to define.

'The next day I was asked to go for a part in a drama-documentary. Franc told me the unbelievable story of this girl. It was like a dream – one of those parts that comes along once or twice in a career.

'I had six weeks to prepare for the role, mostly learning what it was like to be deaf. But I also spent time in Bradford with people who knew Sandra – and we filmed *Dummy* on Lumb Lane, in Bradford, and other real-life places featured in *Band of Gold*. So when I met producer Tony Dennis and director Richard Standeven for *Band of Gold*, I had some experience of that world. But I hadn't a clue about doing a Yorkshire accent. In Bradford we met some women at a working women's centre who were fantastically candid about their lives. It was tremendously helpful.

'My challenge in the first series was to build Rose into a three-dimensional person,' says Geraldine. 'Originally you see Rose as the great bullish boss of the Lane. I felt hugely disliked as Rose. So it was amazing to find out how many viewers really liked her. The part felt very unattractive, but I like playing real characters and I think it is wrong for actors to cut the edge off a character in order to be sympathetic.'

Geraldine, who enjoyed one of her biggest screen successes as Sarah Layton in Granada Television's epic series *The Jewel in the Crown*, had never played the same character for 18 episodes. 'I did, however, do 11 episodes and 13 hours of *The Jewel in the Crown*, but when I started that I had read the book and knew the ending, so I knew where I was heading. With Rose, I headed into the darkness. All I knew was that, by the end of the first series, I would reveal the existence of a child, which interested me.'

Geraldine decided to become an actress while still at boarding school, after discovering she could make people laugh: 'Somebody on the staff saw me larking about and cast me as the Artful Dodger in a school production of *Oliver!* when I was 12. Hearing the audience laugh was a wonderful experience. In schools of that type, where everybody is brilliant, you have to shine, and I *did* shine at acting.'

After leaving school with O-levels and an English A-level, Geraldine worked as a dresser at the Aldwych Theatre, in London, for £4 a week. She later trained at The Drama Centre, in London, and has since won a Critics' Award as Best Actress for her performance in *Dummy*. She has been nominated for a BAFTA award three times – for her roles in *Dummy*, *The Jewel in the Crown* and *Band of Gold*; and her many other television programmes include *The History Man*, *Blott on the Landscape*, *Inspector Morse*, *Doggin' Around*, *Drovers' Gold* and *Rebecca*. Her appearance in Sir Peter Hall's production of *The Merchant of Venice*, in the West End and on Broadway, gained her a both a Drama Desk award and a Tony nomination; while her role in the film *She's Been Away* won her the Venice Film Festival Volpi Cup for Best Actress. Married to film director Jo Blatchley, with whom she has a daughter, Eleanor, Geraldine lives in London.

she is putting on her stockings. She emerges from the bathroom in a black bra and stockings, a short pink dress and black stilettos. She walks up and down the hotel room for him, puts her foot on the seat of his sofa, then walks away. At no time does she make contact. When he is satisfied, she turns round to him, smiles and asks: 'Do I get to keep the shoes?' Later, Curly asks her to 'walk' for him every week, for £150 a time.

As Tracy lies in bed sipping champagne with Tommy, Dez cruises the Lane looking for her. Meanwhile, DCI Newall visits Steve, who refuses to believe that Gina was on the game. 'The fact is, she didn't need her case because she wasn't flogging make-up,' insists the detective.

Carol arrives at Rose's house, fanning herself with £20 notes, and explains that the scratches on Curly's hands were caused by a skin complaint. As Carol leaves, Dez gets out of his car, walks over and knocks on the door. As Rose opens it, Dez charges in: 'So where is she?' he shouts, asking about Tracy. He draws a knife, puts it to her cheek and draws blood. As he drives off, Rose holds a towel to her face.

After Carol arrives home, a car pulls up outside and a man gets out. She goes upstairs, looks in on Emma, then runs a bath. Just as she has stripped to her underwear, a car pulls up outside and a man gets out. Carol puts on her dressing gown and walks downstairs. After putting the chain on the front door, she returns upstairs to the bathroom. Then, as she is soaking in the bath, she sees the door handle turn; the door opens and DCI Newall appears. 'You lied to me,' he says. 'Who's been a naughty girl, then?' He tells Carol that he knows Gina was hustling and also that he knows that she was working with her. Then Newall has sex with Carol in the bathroom, standing up. 'You're still a good screw, then,' he tells her.

As Carol soaks in the bath, she sees the door handle turn; the door opens and Newall appears. 'You lied to me,' he says

As Steve drives to the spot where Gina was murdered, which is still guarded by police, Tracy leaves the hotel and is followed by a car down a back lane. A car door slams shut, her steps quicken, then Tracy is pushed to the ground and hit over the head with a rock. She lies motionless with her eyes open, apparently dead.

Episode Three: Damaged

Steve is interrogated about the murder of his wife, Gina, as Tracy fights for her life in hospital. Her mother refuses to believe that she could have been a prostitute. Steve engineers a confrontation with Carol because Gina teamed up with her on the street. After Anita's flat is raided and both she and Rose are arrested, news comes of another prostitute's murder.

Carol and Rose head for Anita's flat. They try to force their way in, but the chain on the inside stops them and, with the door between them and Anita, they accuse her of shopping Gina. Meanwhile, DCI Newall interrogates Steve, following his visit to the scene of his wife's murder, and asks him if he wants to confess to the crime. 'I didn't kill her!' protests Steve. At that point, Newall hears the news about the attack on Tracy from DS Kershaw, who points out that the tyre tracks at the scene of the crime are different from those in the Gina murder case. Newall then releases Steve.

As Carol walks along the Lane with Rose, Newall pulls up in his car and tells her to get in the back. He takes her to see Tracy in Southpark Hospital, where she is being kept alive. Carol, shaking with fear, tells Newall who Tracy is and gives him the name of her pimp, Dez, who is then taken to the police station for questioning. He denies giving Tracy drugs or putting her on the street. Dez claims that Rose was always threatening Tracy and 'wanted her off the Lane'.

Steve Dixon is Gina Dixon's estranged husband. Married for seven years, he has had little work for the past two years, after being made redundant. His violence led Gina to throw him out of the council house they had bought. Steve was desperate for a reconciliation, though, and acted as a baby-sitter while he believed Gina was selling cosmetics. In reality, she was on the game.

Mr Moore is a debt collector who chased Gina for the money she owed after trying to ease her finances by taking out a single loan to pay off her previous debts. He arrived with a heavy to take away Gina's belongings. When she became hysterical he told her he would be back at the end of the month.

George Ferguson is a loan shark and also the married lover of Anita Braithwaite, for whom he provides a flat. He owns a cleaning business, called Klenzit, and turns out to be the person who took over Gina's loan. He asks Anita to give him a false alibi for the nights of both of the prostitute murders.

Curly is a weird-looking punter who met Carol Johnson in the Hustler's Arms and showed interest in Gina shortly before she died. He became one of Carol's clients, but was only interested in sitting down with rubber gloves on while she 'walked' for him in a G-string and black stockings. He wore the gloves to hide his eczema.

Dez Sadiq is Tracy Richards' evil pimp, who put the schoolgirl on the streets and provides her with drugs. Determined to keep a tight rein on Tracy and stop her joining forces with the other women, who befriended her after the murder of prostitute Gina Dixon, he threatened Carol and drew blood as he held a knife to Rose's cheek.

Ian is one of tragic Gina's first clients, and Carol stole £50 from his mantelpiece while Gina was having sex with him in his bedroom. Ian claimed to be 'in security', but later he is seen at the leisure centre for which the prostitutes hope to win a cleaning contract in an attempt to get off the game.

At the Hustler's Arms, Carol and Rose corner Anita in the toilet. Anita insists she was only trying to help the police to find Gina's killer. Carol and Rose then tell her that Tracy is in hospital. As the three of them walk along the Lane towards Anita's flat, DC Jameson pulls up in his police car and takes Rose in for questioning. Meanwhile, DS Kershaw and PC Derbyshire have tracked down Tracy's parents in Harrogate. 'Have you found Naomi?' asks Mrs Richards as she answers the door to them.

Mr Moore confronts Steve in the street outside Gina's house to point out that her loan still has to be repaid. Inside, Joyce is tidying up; Steve goes in and tells her he has been at the police station all night. 'They think I've killed her,' he says, adding that Gina was a prostitute. Joyce refuses to believe this and the pair end up having a fierce argument. When Steve goes to Joanne's school to pick her up, he spots Carol collecting Emma and wonders whether Gina was working with her.

Mrs Richards arrives at the hospital and confirms that the attack victim is her daughter. Meanwhile, DCI Newall is questioning Rose at the police station. He suggests that she tried to get rid of Tracy because the young prostitutes were taking work away from the older women working the Lane. Rose admits to trying to frighten Tracy off, but says that Dez threatened to slit open her face with a knife if she didn't tell him where Tracy was, and that she had told him Tracy was at the hotel.

In the Hustler's Arms, Carol is joined by Curly: 'This £150 – when do I get it?' she asks. He tells her that she can either have £150, if they go back to her house, or £100, if they use a hotel. By now, Dez is once more being questioned by Newall, who tells him about the knife wound on Rose's face. 'We know that you did it,' claims Newall, adding that they simply needed to find the weapon. 'I just wanted to frighten her – that's all,' Dez admits. 'I just wanted to show her what would happen if she went with them. I didn't hit her that hard.'

Rose, who is feeling guilty, is sitting at Tracy's bedside in hospital. The tracheotomy has been removed from her throat and a small dressing covers the wound. Mrs Richards walks in and asks Rose: 'Did Naomi work with you?' Tracy's mother does not attempt to conceal her disgust and refuses to believe that her daughter would be capable of selling her body. 'We gave her everything,' says Mrs Richards. Rose reveals that her own child was

taken away from her at the age of two months: 'They said I weren't fit to look after her.'

As Curly leaves Carol's house, Steve watches from his parked car. Convinced that Carol led his wife astray, Steve gets out of the car, walks over to the house and looks in through the kitchen window. Then Carol leaves the house, too, and walks to the local off-licence. Steve follows her, starts talking to her and pays for her bottle of brandy. Thinking that he is a punter, she takes him back to her house and asks him for £20. Then Steve starts questioning Carol about how much Gina charged and she admits to having known Gina for a short time. Steve, confessing to being Gina's husband, asks: 'So what does it feel like to be a whore?' Carol refuses his money and they struggle – Steve rams the cash into her mouth and leaves.

'She was a whore,' Steve says of his murdered wife. 'And that's why you killed her,' Newall retorts

In response to a desperate phone call from Carol, Newall arrives – it emerges that he had previously been transferred from the vice squad because of his relationship with her. When Carol tells Newall about Steve, he rushes off and confronts Steve at his house. Newall strikes him and a struggle follows. 'She was a whore,' Steve says of his murdered wife. 'And that's why you killed her,' Newall retorts.

Two policemen raid Anita's house as Rose entertains a client. They accuse Anita of running a brothel and take Rose and Anita to the police station; they arrive just as Newall is walking in with Steve. DC Jameson tells his boss that another body has been found in an alley off Mannering Lane, in the red-light district. It turns out to be that of another prostitute, Amanda Smeaton, who resembles Carol. The corpse is put in a body bag and the area is cordoned off.

Meanwhile, at the hospital, Tracy finally wakes up and sees her mother sleeping next to her bed.

Tracy's middle-class parents, Helen and Tim (who abused his daughter when she was just 11 years old) visit Naomi – her real name – in hospital

Episode Four: Revenge

Tracy returns to her parents' home in Harrogate after leaving hospital, but runs off again, having told her mother that her father sexually abused her years earlier. She is also stunned to discover that it was Dez who had assaulted her. George admits to Anita that he is seeing another woman and throws her out of the flat. As Carol's paranoia reaches its height, she finally cracks and takes her revenge on Curly. Meanwhile, Rose – determined to give up prostitution – sets off for London, followed by Tracy.

Tracy has a disturbing dream at the hospital. Her mother, father, Rose, Carol, Anita, Dez, sister Laura and Tommy from the hotel all appear in a ring around her, singing 'The farmer's in his den...'

Tracy screams and sits bolt upright in her bed. Her mother reassures her, and Tracy, whose health is improving, is moved to a side ward.

Meanwhile, two uniformed police officers stop George Ferguson in his car and search it. 'There must be thousands of red Jags,' he says. 'What are you going to do – track them all down?' But DC Jameson discovers Anita's black bags and bleach, and takes George in for questioning. When Jameson says the car's registration number matches that of a car seen parked off Mannering Lane the previous night, George finally admits that he was there. Then he is asked where he was on the night of Gina Dixon's murder.

Rose is fined £300 in the magistrate's court following the raid on Anita's flat. Tracy's father arrives

CATHY TYSON
AS CAROL

Carol Johnson went on the game at 13, and had a nervous breakdown after a serial killer started murdering prostitutes. Cathy Tyson knows all about fear and the art of survival on the streets – the grim realities of growing up in Toxteth, the area of Liverpool scarred by riots in the early 1980s. An only child, Cathy was brought up single-handedly by her mother, a white social worker, after her father, a West Indian lawyer, walked out and returned to Trinidad. And she was used to violence and racial abuse.

'My mother was a professional, so we weren't poor,' says Cathy. 'We had money and holidays, and never went hungry. But I didn't have any brothers or sisters, so I had to fight my own battles. A lot of children round our way didn't have fathers, either. In the white part of Liverpool 8 it was common to be called "nigger". Once I was being taunted by a boy and his mates, so I went over and battered him. I rarely did that, but I just had to stop him.

'I remember thinking: "Is that what it takes to get respect? Standing up and fighting?" I cried about what happened. That boy was in pain, but he never did it again. When you grow up and achieve success, all that drains away. Nobody's going to call me "nigger" now. But it's still there for the young kids.'

Cathy left school at the age of 16 and set out to become an actress. After attending the Rathbone Theatre Workshop on a government training scheme, she went to drama college. Her professional career started at the Everyman Theatre, Liverpool, where she made her début in *The Liverpool Blitz Show* and later played Ophelia in *Hamlet*. She also performed with the RSC for two years.

Cathy's big break came when she starred as high-class hooker Simone, with Bob Hoskins, in the 1986 film *Mona Lisa*. However, despite its success the starring roles that many had predicted just didn't come along. She turned down many similar roles and let acting take a back seat, following her wedding to actor Craig Charles and the birth of their son Jack. The marriage finished after five years, but Cathy does not rule out marrying again, though she concedes it's hard having a family as well as being an actor. 'I have help now,' she says, 'and sometimes I turn down work to be with Jack. And after I've worked for a while, I take time off.'

Cathy appeared in numerous programmes before *Band of Gold* brought her lasting television fame. One of the earliest was Alan Bleasdale's *Scully*, in which she played Joanna, whom the schoolboy football fanatic of the title fancied. Cathy also acted on screen in *The Practice*, *Chancer*, *The Lenny Henry Show*, *Rules of Engagement*, *The Lost Language of Cranes*, *Angels*, the Granada Television play *Medics*, *Out of the Blue* and an episode of the Michael Elphick series *Harry*, in which she played an HIV counsellor working with prostitutes. Cathy also appeared in the 1994 BBC cinema film *Priest*, written by Jimmy McGovern, as the housekeeper to a gay priest.

Cathy was flattered by the offer to play Carol. 'Kay had me in mind for the role even without seeing me in *Mona Lisa*, which surprised me,' says Cathy. 'Because of my previous role, it was a big decision to take it on, but my agent was really positive about Carol's complex and obsessive character, which had more flesh than Simone in *Mona Lisa*.'

After the second series of *Band of Gold*, Cathy toured with David Schofield (DCI Newall) in a stage production of *The Merchant of Venice*. She also played a barrister in *Brothers and Sisters*, a 10-week serial about life in black Britain, and is in demand for documentary voice-overs. Away from work, she enjoys reading black literature: 'The history of our country isn't told very well,' she says. 'All the history taught in school is about queens and kings and "great white men", but there are so many stories that still have to be told.'

Rose, Carol and Anita are the guardian angels in Tracy's disturbing dream as she lies in hospital after being hit over the head with a rock and left for dead

at the hospital from London, and DCI Newall asks Tracy to make a statement about the attack on her. Curly turns up at Carol's house while Rose and Anita are there, saying that he was worried about her after newspaper reports of the latest murder. He adds that he originally thought the blurred photograph in the paper was of Carol.

Rose goes to the hospital armed with a bunch of flowers, sees Tracy giving a statement to Newall and walks away, throwing the flowers in a waste bin. After Tracy tells Newall that she was at the hotel to protect Carol, he goes straight to Carol's house and threatens to take her in for prostitution.

She points out that when he had been in the vice squad she let him have 'free shags' in return for being left alone. Later, Carol starts to become paranoid, thinking that she is being followed as she walks down the street – but the man walking behind her is just from the water board.

George visits Anita and asks her to give him an alibi for the night that Gina Dixon was killed. Then he listens from her bedroom as she tells Newall and Kershaw that George was with her on the nights of both murders. However, Newall reveals that her flat was under surveillance the previous day and there was no sign of George entering or leaving. But Anita insists he was there. After the detectives leave, George tells Anita she has landed them both in trouble. She points out he was not really with her on the night of Gina's murder and that he followed Gina after she left the flat.

Debt collector Mr Moore confronts Steve outside his house, telling him that Gina owed more than £1,000 on her loan, that she had put the house up as collateral and that £180 is due at the end of the month. Meanwhile, Tracy leaves hospital with her parents and is besieged by newspaper reporters and photographers. Watching these scenes on the television news, Anita tells Carol and Rose that she is confused: Curly, Dez and George are all suspects. She admits that George was not with her on the night of either murder and Rose insists that Anita must tell the police.

Back at her parents' home in Harrogate, Tracy sits at the dining room table with her younger sister, Laura, who tells her that she prayed that Tracy would die after newspapers reported that she was a prostitute. At Turton Lane Police Station, a tearful Anita admits to Newall and Kershaw that George had not been with her on the night of Amanda Smeaton's murder, and that he had left soon after Gina on the night of her murder. As a result, George is pulled in for questioning. At the cemetery, Carol finds a card next to Gina's plaque: it reads 'Sinner'. She then sees a man watching her. She nearly jumps out of her skin when Joyce walks up and asks: 'Are you Emma's mam?' Carol explains about the man, but he has disappeared.

Tracy's mother, Helen, decides not to attend her regular therapy session on her daughter's first night back home. Her husband, Tim, suspects that she is beginning to believe Tracy's former allegations of being sexually abused by him.

There is a shock for Anita when George returns to her flat from the police station and tells her he had an alibi on the night of both murders – a new girlfriend of a couple of months. 'I didn't want to tell you because I felt sorry for you,' he says, adding that their affair is over.

A red Mercedes with mirrored windows stops on the Lane: the window slides down and Rose looks in, asking the driver whether he is looking for a 'nice time'. 'Do I get it cheaper because you're a bit older?' is the reply. She turns down his offer to get into the car and catches sight of her over-made-up face staring from the mirrored window; she wipes the lipstick off her mouth. Later, sitting in the Hustler's Arms with Carol, Rose says: 'I think I'm gonna bugger off…There's nowt doin' for me here. I'm finished on the Lane.'

Carol, by now convinced that she is being followed, leaves the pub and becomes aware of footsteps behind her as she walks down the Lane. As she walks faster, they quicken. She then turns round and faces the man. 'I'm looking for someone,' he says. On seeing her alarm, he walks away. When Carol arrives back at her house, she turns the corner and bumps into Curly, who is there for his weekly session. By now, her nerves are raw.

Anita arrives home to find that Mr Moore and a locksmith are changing the locks on her flat, and that her belongings are stacked outside in four black plastic bags. When Tracy leaves home without telling her parents, her mother drives around looking for her, finally discovering her running down a road in the pouring rain. She gets out and asks where she is going. 'I sold myself when I was 11,' replies Tracy. 'I got a new pair of trainers for playing piggy-backs with daddy…He put his hands down my knickers.' Tracy walks away. She goes to Dez's house, where a teenage girl called Sarah tells her that he is in Wakefield Prison. 'They said he hit some lass over the head,' says Sarah. Tracy walks away, stunned and in tears when she realizes that Dez was her attacker.

'I sold myself when I was 11,' replies Tracy. 'I got a new pair of trainers for playing piggy-backs with daddy'

After magistrates fine Rose £300 following the police raid on Anita's flat, she feels it is time to change her life; she makes the decision to move to London and better herself

At Carol's house, Curly puts the usual black stockings and stilettos on a work surface, in anticipation of her 'walking' for him. 'Not on there, stupid!' she screams, pouring bleach on the top and scrubbing away maniacally with a cloth. She then gets irritated with Curly for taking so long to satisfy himself. He asks her to say 'something dirty', and, reaching breaking point, she tells him: 'I know what'll make you feel better.' Carol takes Curly to her bedroom for the first time.

Curly laughs nervously as she handcuffs him to the bed, ties his feet together with the stockings, unbuttons his shirt and removes his trousers. A whistle comes from the kitchen – Carol fetches a boiling kettle, sits astride Curly on the bed, holds the kettle above him and says, 'You're goin' to be all nice and clean,' as she pours the boiling water over his genitals. His screams are deafening.

Meanwhile, Rose boards a train for London, determined to start her life anew. She is already on the train at Bradford Railway Station when Tracy runs along the platform and joins her. They both laugh as the train pulls out of the station.

Episode Five: Told

Rose and Tracy settle down to their new life in London: Tracy continues on the game and becomes more involved with drugs; and Rose takes a business course and falls for Richard. Carol prepares to leave a secure psychiatric unit after suffering a nervous breakdown and going through the trauma of seeing her daughter, Emma, being taken into care. When debt collector Mr Moore turns out to be just a front man for George Ferguson – who took over Gina's loan – Anita moves in with Carol and plots her revenge.

Tracy wanders through the bright lights of Soho, chatting to nightclub doormen and prostitutes. With a trendier, more expensive look, she walks into the Blue Gardenia Club and puts a card advertising 'Tracy Wild Child New Model' on the wall near a telephone, bins other prostitutes' cards and goes up to the bar. She notices two men who are eyeing her up and walks over to them.

Meanwhile, at Highfield Psychiatric Secure Unit, Carol is showering and starts to wash her hair. On hearing a noise, she opens the shower curtain and finds a male patient standing there in front of her. They both scream. Later, in an assessment session with social worker Anne Devlin, key worker Rob Jones, psychiatrist Eileen Whittaker and community nurse Janet McCullough, Carol is asked whether she will be able to manage if she goes home the next day, as planned: 'I managed before I came in,' she says.

Asked about her breakdown, Carol says that she thought someone was watching her all the time, probably because of the murders. She remembers that her obsession with cleaning meant that she used to get through three bottles of bleach and a large bottle of disinfectant every week: 'I reckon I must have been goin' off my head,' she adds. Afterwards, during a visit from Anita, Carol is told that she can leave the next day.

Rose, looking different in T-shirt and jeans, is taking a business course at a further education college. She becomes exasperated and accidentally disconnects other students' machines. Visiting a drop-in centre, she tells Richard of her frustration. 'You talked me into doin' the bloody course,' she says. But he convinces her to continue with it and she promises to cook him a curry. Tracy arrives, sets off with Rose for their flat – it is close to a busy railway line – and tells her that she has a client arriving later. As they eat dinner, back at the flat, Tracy tells Rose that Richard is just a 'do-gooder', but Rose replies that he helped her to get on the course.

After social worker Anne Devlin has taken Carol home, Anita tells Carol that she has been thrown out of Rose's flat by the landlord and that she has brought all her belongings with her in black bin liners. Then, DCI Newall turns up and tells Carol that Curly will not be pressing charges. Unnerved by his presence, she starts cleaning her kitchen work surfaces: 'I'm packin' the Lane in,' she says, adding that she will 'go back on the social' or get a job. Carol berates Newall for failing to catch the murderer and claims it could be Moore, the debt collector,

Newall and his men break down the door of Moore's flat and find him in bed with a young man. 'You'd better start talking,' Newall tells Moore, 'otherwise that rent boy's going to be using Grecian 2000 by the time you get out.'

Meanwhile, Carol goes to Emma's school to watch her daughter leave for the day and be met by her foster mother. Joyce arrives to find her in tears: 'I've just seen her bein' picked up,' says Carol. 'She seemed happy without me.'

Later, Carol smooches with Newall on her sofa. He tells her that Moore has been charged with indecent assault on a rent boy, but that he is not the murderer. In any case, Moore was only a front-man for George Ferguson, who was the loan shark to whom Gina owed money. Then Anita walks in and Newall leaves.

In London, Richard joins Rose and Tracy for dinner at their flat. Tracy is antagonistic and goes off to the the kitchen; Rose follows her and they argue. Afterwards, back in the living room, Richard tells Rose about his ex-wife, Jane, who left him for another man two years earlier. When he asks to stay the night, Rose finds it difficult to enjoy sex with him because part of her is shut off. She does, however, become gradually more passionate and is eventually satisfied sexually for the first time with a man. Then Tracy arrives home from the Blue Gardenia Club, where she has bought some tablets, and puts one of her cards into Richard's jacket pocket.

Rose finds it difficult to enjoy sex with Richard but gradually becomes more passionate

Carol and Anita arrive at Joyce's house, where her partner Bob – a client – is shocked to see them and makes an excuse so that he can leave the room. Carol tells Anita that they have 'all done him'. Later, while Joyce is waiting for a prescription for her granddaughter, Sarah, Anita lets on that 'everybody did' her boyfriend.

Tracy tells Rose that she is worried that she will dump her for Richard, who then phones, having found Tracy's card in his jacket. Tracy tells Rose that the caller wants 'two of us' to go along, but does not reveal his identity, which Tracy has guessed. Rose refuses, saying that unless she gives up prostitution she will end up 'doin' blow jobs for half o' lager and a bag o' chips'. Later, Tracy phones Richard to arrange a meeting, and says that her friend has agreed to come along. Devastated, Richard takes a taxi to the appointed meeting place, but he spots Tracy with another prostitute, and, relieved, he asks the taxi-driver to drive him back to Lambeth.

In Bradford, Carol tells her social worker that she will be looking for a job 'next week' and that Anita is staying only until the following day. Meanwhile, Joyce empties Bob's clothes out of a dressing table and puts them in a suitcase. She discovers a scrapbook with newspaper cuttings about the murders, and when Bob walks in she starts to rip it up, before throwing the suitcase at him and telling him to leave.

Rose is encouraged to take a business course in London by Richard, who runs a drop-in centre; the couple become close and Rose confides the secret that she had a daughter taken away for adoption as a baby

Two hundred miles away, Richard visits Rose at her college and says that he wants to talk. As they walk in Trafalgar Square, he tells her that he had found Tracy's card in his pocket and phoned, asking if she could bring a friend along. He admits that he thought that Rose might be a prostitute. 'I'm really sorry you couldn't just come straight out and ask me 'cause I'd have told you I've given it up,' she says.

Bent on revenge, Anita visits George Ferguson's wife, Kathleen, and tells her that she had been having an affair with her husband until two months previously. She adds that George is a loan shark: 'He threatened Gina Dixon and frightened her on to the Lane and that's why she ended up dead,' says Anita. At that, Kathleen finally lets Anita into the house.

In London, Rose tells Richard about her daughter, Hannah, whom she used to think about while having sex to take her mind off what was happening. Rose explains that she had given birth to Hannah when she was 16; the father, Paul Ramsden, was just a year older and the baby was taken away from her after less than two months. Shortly afterwards, she became a prostitute on the Lane. Back at the drop-in centre, Richard tells Rose that he will need a couple of weeks to 'think the whole thing through properly' and asks when she last had a blood test. 'I've had three blood tests,' she tells him and, as she walks out, adds: 'I could really have loved you.'

Meanwhile, Joyce tells Carol that she has been a cleaner since Gina was three, but she will now tell George Ferguson that she is giving up her job. She plans to apply to the council for a cleaning contract at the local leisure centre. Carol agrees to team up with her.

After being allowed to visit her daughter, Emma, and her foster parents, a tearful Carol walks home along the Lane. A car pulls up and the driver, Ian – the client whom Carol had robbed while he had sex with Gina – reminds her that he had promised to take her and Gina for a drink. Alarmed, Carol runs off to see Newall at the police

Tracy tries to wreck Rose's relationship with Richard by putting her 'Wild Child' card into his jacket pocket

station. He tells her that Ian, too, has only just left hospital and hints that she is being hysterical.

Realizing how Tracy has ruined her relationship with Richard, Rose calls her a 'scheming little bitch' and slaps her across the face. But as Rose packs her case, Tracy pleads with her not to go, saying she does not want to leave London. Rose simply replies that she will go without Tracy if she will not come.

While Rose catches her train north, Tracy visits Richard at the drop-in centre and tells Richard that Rose is returning to Yorkshire and, probably, to the Lane. Tracy says it is 'sad that Rose ever had to meet you', before visiting the Blue Gardenia Club, knocking over champagne glasses on the bar and smashing a large mirror with a stool.

Meanwhile, Carol returns to her house and, as she approaches the front door, turns round, aware that she is being watched …

Episode Six: Clean

Rose arrives back in Bradford and moves in with Carol, who is finally allowed to have Emma back. They join Joyce and Anita to make a bid for the cleaning contract at the leisure centre, which they hope would give them all a job and a real chance to keep them off the game. George's wife, Kathleen, agrees to finance their business and locks George out of their house. A meeting for Carol at the leisure centre brings her face-to-face with the killer…

As Carol lies asleep in bed, she is woken by tapping at her bedroom window. She grabs a bread knife from her bedside cabinet, creeps down the stairs, opens her outside door – and finds Rose, who has arrived back from London with her suitcase: 'I've been lobbing boulders at you for the past half-hour,' says Rose. 'I thought you must be dead.'

In London, Tracy picks herself up from the gutter outside the Blue Gardenia Club and discovers that she has been robbed. But Ronnie, from the club, finds Tracy and takes her under his wing. He gives her some money and, when she asks what he wants for it in return, he replies, 'Have it on me.'

Meanwhile, Rose tells Carol that she had given up hustling and that Tracy was making money but 'blowing most of it on crack'. Later, Carol mops up the kitchen floor as Joyce arrives with two of her grandchildren and asks her to look after them while she goes to work. Carol steps outside the house, where she is being watched by someone in a car with a video camera.

At George Ferguson's house, his wife Kathleen asks if he would like to eat out that evening, but he says that he always goes to the club on Thursdays. Meanwhile, Carol and Rose take Joyce's two younger grandchildren to school to pick up Joanne and see Carol's daughter, Emma. When Carol suggests that she might simply take Emma away with her, Rose insists that she must go through the proper procedures.

At the offices of Klenzit, George's cleaning company, George tells Joyce that he would like her to manage the leisure centre cleaning contract for which he is bidding, and says he would increase her wages. Then Joyce tells Gloria, a fellow-cleaner, about her plans to bid for the contract herself. Later, as Joyce, Carol, Rose and Anita talk about the contract and fill in a questionnaire, social worker Anne Devlin arrives. Carol tells her that she wants Emma back.

That evening, Carol's black-and-white-striped top is taken from her washing line. Later, the top is cut to shreds with a sharp knife in someone's house – alongside a photograph of Carol wearing it and newspaper cuttings about the murders.

The following day, Joyce, Carol, Rose and Anita take a taxi-ride to the Town Hall for their interview with a panel from the council, headed by leisure centre manager Mrs Minkin and including one of their clients, Councillor Baker. They explain that they chose Scrubbit International as their company name to show they 'weren't small-time'. But Mrs Minkin points out that completing a business course and operating an £80,000 contract 'are not the same thing'. Feeling dejected after Mrs Minkin's comments, the women leave, but Rose is determined to carry on. Then Councillor Baker tells Ferguson about the meeting and says that the women 'know things' about him. Ferguson is adamant that the women must not get the contract.

After a bank manager refuses the women a loan, stating that they have 'no management

That evening, Carol's black-and-white-striped top is taken from her washing line and is later cut to shreds with a knife

experience, no business plan…and absolutely no collateral', Anita visits Kathleen Ferguson and tells her how she is planning to get her own back on George.

Carol and Rose arrive back at Carol's house and find a bouquet of dead flowers on the doorstep, bearing the message 'Sinner'. As they walk in, the phone rings; Carol answers, and hears the word 'Sinner' whispered.

When Carol visits Joyce, Steve storms out. 'You're mixin' wi' scum, Joyce,' he tells his mother-in-law, and an argument follows. Later, Steve apologizes to Joyce and tells her that he is taking a job in Scarborough.

In London, Richard arrives at Tracy's flat and gives her a note to pass on to Rose. Back in Bradford, Carol, Rose and Anita sit talking dispiritedly, convinced they have lost the cleaning contract. Then, the telephone rings: it is Kathleen Ferguson, who asks to speak to Anita and tells her

that she will provide the backing for the women.

The following day, Anne Devlin arrives at Carol's house with Emma for a day-visit. When Emma leaves, the social worker tells Carol that her daughter will soon be back for good.

Meanwhile, two teenagers break into the house in which Carol's top was cut up, and they spot photographs of the murder victims pinned to the wall of the study.

At the leisure centre, Councillor Baker tells the women that they should forget about the cleaning contract, but they reply that Kathleen Ferguson is backing them. He phones George on his mobile telephone with the news, just as George is arriving home to find that his wife has changed the locks on the front door.

As Tracy arrives at the Hustler's Arms, looking for Rose, Ian pulls up outside his house. Seeing the police there – who have been tipped off by the teenagers – he drives off at speed.

Tracy, earning good money in London and buying expensive clothes, but getting deeper into drugs, picks herself up from the gutter to be taken under the wing of Ronnie from the Blue Gardenia Club

Anita, Joyce, Rose and Carol seek a new future by applying for the cleaning contract at the council's leisure centre, in competition with shady businessman George Ferguson, Anita's ex-lover

Carol walks out of her house, and Curly gives her a shock by tapping her on the shoulder. She apologizes for what had happened previously and tells him that she is off the game, but Curly says he needs her to 'walk' for him. Carol tells him to stop hassling her and steps into a taxi for an appointment with Councillor Baker at the leisure centre.

DCI Newall looks round Ian's house and studies the photographs pinned on the wall; he also watches a video of dead prostitute Amanda Smeaton – who bore a resemblance to Carol – and of Carol outside her house. Then, he rushes to the Lane. Meanwhile, Rose, Anita and Joyce arrive at the Hustler's Arms.

Ian watches Carol on the security video as she walks around the leisure centre looking for Councillor Baker. She looks out of a window and sees him drive away in his car. Then the lights go out as she walks past the swimming pool. Carol starts running but finds that the outside doors have

been locked – Ian explains that he has not released the lock. She is relieved, until he adds: 'Did you get the flowers?' She runs away from him. 'There's no point in running – there's nowhere to go,' Ian says. Carol gets into a lift and stops Ian from entering by kicking him in the groin. She is shocked to find that there is a dead man in the lift.

Arriving at a gallery above the swimming pool, Carol is confronted once more by Ian. 'I've given up the Lane...I'm not a hustler any more,' she pleads. 'You stole money from me,' he retorts.' Ian explains that he murdered Amanda Smeaton – 'the wrong girl' – because of Carol and that it is now her turn. Carol leaps from the gallery into the pool.

Outside, a taxi pulls up and Rose, Anita and Joyce get out. Tracy, already there, screams: 'He's killin' Carol.' Ian is now pushing Carol, who cannot swim, under the water. The women break in and Joyce hits Ian in the back with a fire extinguisher and he falls into the water. They pull Carol out of the pool and Joyce revives her, while Rose rescues Ian from the pool. Carol comes round to find Curly looking at her. 'Oh, Jesus, I've landed in hell,' she says.

Later, in the Hustler's Arms, Tracy screws up the note from Richard and tells Rose that she is not staying. Newall is told that it was the women who were responsible for capturing Ian. Newall says he will be moved on and asks Carol to go with him. 'How long do you think we'd last?' she says. The detective adds that the fraud squad had been investigating Ferguson for the previous two months. The women, realizing that they could land the cleaning contract, make a toast to Gina. Then Curly enters, and the band of women fall around in fits of hysterical laughter.

WHAT THE PAPERS SAID

'The first episode of Kay Mellor's pacy new six-part drama serial about girls on the game in Yorkshire Ripper territory could hardly be accused of plugging prostitution as a career opportunity for cash-strapped housewives: it ended with the murder of one such absolute beginner.

'There was nothing remotely titillating here, unless you counted the excellent Cathy Tyson's thigh-high wading boots that made her look as if she were going fishing … for men. Geraldine James is already great value as a highly territorial old pro who enjoys a nice handbag brawl in a pub. She, however, is the milk of human kindness in comparison with the vicious Asian pimp who threatens the women with a knife.

'Mellor's bleak script sees women as perpetual victims of men in one way or another. Newcomer Ruth Gemmell was impressive as Gina, a proud young mother separated from her violent husband and trying to pay off the loan shark with a little secret street-walking.'
Maureen Paton, *Daily Express*

Just about every performance is high quality. Geraldine James, Barbara Dickson and Cathy Tyson are excellent while Samantha Morton is a star of the future…Kay Mellor's uncompromising script gives this dynamic drama its unmissable edge…It is the best new drama of the year.'
Stafford Hildred, *The Sun*

The remarkable Ms Mellor's meticulously researched story has such a convincing documentary feel that I found myself noting down the killer's car number so I could phone *Crimewatch UK*. The thing that sets it apart…is the conviction that we are in the presence of a truly great performance from Cathy Tyson as Carol, poor Gina's teacher and avenger. She is mesmerizing.'
Margaret Forwood, *Daily Express*

'Kay Mellor's scripts brought forth powerful and courageous performances…Men, it must be said, did not emerge well. As a sex we were either pimps, policemen or pathetic.'
Matthew Bond, *The Times*

4

Band of Gold 2

Such was the overwhelming success of the first series of *Band of Gold* that, after just two episodes had been broadcast, Granada Television commissioned Kay Mellor to write a second series. But, at first, she was unsure whether she had anything new to write about. Then she was put on the spot at executive producer Sally Head's house: 'So what is the second series going to be, Kay?' Sally asked. 'I just heard myself saying that, more than anything, it was about Tracy. I wanted to return to the image that had so fascinated me when I saw that young girl on the Lane, back at the beginning; it cried out to me that this is what will happen to us as a society, if we don't look after our children.'

Another influence on Kay's ideas for the second series was West Yorkshire Chief Constable Keith Hellawell, who had met the writer on a

Carol, Rose and Anita keep off the streets in the second series of *Band of Gold* by running a cleaning co-operative regional television programme and asked her to tackle the issue of crack cocaine. It was just after 18-year-old prostitute Maureen Stepan had been found murdered in a crack-related incident in Bradford's red-light district – she was discovered by police with her throat slit in a house that had a mattress on the floor and spent condoms in a waste-paper bin; and the body was surrounded by drug paraphernalia.

Over the same weekend that Maureen's body was found, rioting Muslim vigilantes, armed with bricks, stones and petrol bombs, clashed with police after trying to drive prostitutes out of the Manningham district of Bradford. The scenes of violence led some people to blame *Band of Gold* for giving the area a bad reputation and causing more prostitutes to move there. But, as Kay Mellor pointed-ed out, the prostitutes in Lumb Lane were there long before the Muslim community. She was also concerned that the violence had deflected from the issue of women's safety, and she found an ally in West Yorkshire's Chief Constable.

'I found myself on a television panel with Keith Hellawell,' remembers Kay, 'and he told me that crack was not only killing the Lane it was killing all the young people. I'm proud that *Band of Gold* caused a lot of discussion and that I became involved in hundred of debates and chat-shows. Sometimes I would be in a room with a priest at one end and prostitutes at the other, together with police officers and social workers. We would talk about how we could protect our young people and make the environment a safer one for prostitutes, and how to decriminalize prostitution. It's ludicrous that you can be charged with being a prostitute for carrying a condom, and that two women who are working together can be deemed to be running a brothel. There are huge contradictions in the law and it's time that they were thoroughly investigated.'

One of the most memorable images of the second series was the way in which teenager Tracy teamed up with new girl Colette, who wore bondage gear, specialized in sadomasochistic sex and introduced the susceptible girl to the drug culture. They were seen smoking 'rocks' of crack together and having a lesbian relationship. Colette's character also enabled Kay to introduce friction between Tracy and Rose, who had formed an alliance in the first series after Rose took Tracy under her wing following the murder of Gina Dixon.

'I wanted Colette to link into Tracy's story,' says Kay, 'and also to look at lesbianism among prostitutes. A lot of prostitutes are gay or become lesbians because of their experiences through prostitution, in which the male–female contract suddenly becomes work. That makes perfect sense to me. What I don't understand is how prostitutes can have a normal *heterosexual* relationship. Many have sexual problems – this was touched on in the first series, when Rose went to bed with Richard.'

'I'm proud that Band of Gold *caused a lot of discussion and that I became involved in debates'*

With the help of Granada Television, Kay researched the subject of drugs by speaking to addicts in London, Leeds and Birmingham, as well as to drug pushers and to a reformed addict who travelled around London helping others. 'He told me how he got into crack and what the feeling was like,' Kay recalls. 'He explained scientifically what happens to your body when you take it, showed me the substance itself and demonstrated how to make a pipe. He hadn't taken crack himself for four years.'

By the same token, the introduction of Colette meant that sadomasochism had also to be researched. Geraldine James and Sally Head visited the madam of a London sadomasochism parlour and discovered that such places made up a surprisingly large part of the sex industry. 'Men who visit prostitutes often want something other than straight sex,' explains Kay. 'It's something they daren't ask of their wives or partners. I wondered what the extremes were, and decided to push that area, in order to understand the punters and work out what makes them go to prostitutes in the first place.'

Geraldine James, Cathy Tyson, Barbara Dickson and Samantha Morton all returned for the second series, to be joined by Lena Headey as Colette. Because many of Colette's scenes involved her relationship with Tracy, Samantha Morton was asked to read with Lena Headey at her audition. 'She and Sam got on wonderfully,' recalls casting director Carolyn Bartlett. 'It was a slightly offbeat bit of casting, because Lena was already established as a leading screen actress in her own right, but had never been seen in this sort of part. It surprised a lot of people that she not only took the role but played it superbly.'

As Tracy and Colette headed down the road to disaster, the other women tried to leave prostitution behind them. They teamed up with tragic Gina's mother, Joyce Webster, and started a cleaning co-operative called Scrubbit after winning the leisure-centre contract featured in the story at the end of the first series. But distractions came thick and fast: Anita was injured in a hit-and-run incident; Rose searched for her long-lost daughter; and another series of murders began. This time, the identity of the murderer was to shock even them.

Anita's accident at the end of episode one, in which former lover George Ferguson drives straight at her in his Jaguar and leaves her for dead, was staged by stunt co-ordinator Stuart St Paul, with stuntwoman Thérèse Donnelly standing in for Barbara Dickson. 'I wanted to make that quite special,' says Stuart. 'It's very frightening to have a car coming towards you, but Thérèse is a good stuntwoman and we had a couple of spare windscreens and bonnets for the Jag, so I took the risk of teaching her how to go over the bonnet on the day of filming. I was in jeans and a T-shirt, without any pads on. I did the stunt myself eight times to show Thérèse how to do it.

Stuntwoman Thérèse Donnelly stood in for Barbara Dickson in a horrifying scene in which Anita is run over by her avenging former lover, George Ferguson, in his Jaguar

Tony Doyle (as George Ferguson), **David Schofield** (DCI Newall), **Richard Moore** (Curly) and **Ahsen Bhatti** (Dez Sadiq) all returned for the second series of *Band of Gold*. **Rachel Davies** (Joyce Webster) and **Ray Stevenson** (Steve Dixon) also resumed their roles as, respectively, Gina Dixon's mother and widowed husband, this time brought together by their shared grief.

Peter Firth played new character Brian Roberts, the private detective hired by Rose to search for her daughter, Hannah. The Bradford-born actor first appeared on television as a child in series such as *The Double Deckers*. Previously, his best-known screen roles had been in the TV play *The Flipside of Dominick Hyde* and the film *Letter to Brezhnev*.

Jane Cameron, also born in Bradford, played Hannah's adoptive sister, Sarah Levison, whom Brian Roberts tracked down and whom Rose travelled to Manchester to see. Jane Cameron, had recently left drama school and went on to join *Emmerdale* as nanny Sophie Wright, who had a lesbian relationship with Zoë Tate.

Anita Carey, later seen in *Coronation Street* as cleaner Joyce Smedley, mother of Judy Mallett (played by Kay Mellor's daughter, Gaynor Faye), acted leisure centre manager Mrs Minkin. Anita was previously best known as Pat Partington in the sitcom *I Didn't Know You Cared*. She also played Mrs Minkin in the last episode of *Band of Gold*'s first series.

Adam Kotz took the role of Curly's nephew, Vinnie Marshall. Adam has made numerous guest appearances in series such as *Heartbeat*, *The Bill*, *Moving Story*, *Casualty* and *Dangerfield*.

Rebecca Callard, actress daughter of *Coronation Street* star Beverley (Liz McDonald), had a small role as 'sweetie girl' Tula, seen soliciting on the Lane. Rebecca had already made a name for herself as Arrietty in *The Borrowers* and Lucy Cornwell in *Bonjour la Classe*. She has since appeared in *Plotlands* and *The Grand*.

David Bradley, fresh from his role as Labour MP Eddie Wells in *Our Friends in the North*, played drugs baron Alf, calling in his debts from George Ferguson.

Jane Hazlegrove played DC Turner, who interrogated Colette. She played Sue Clayton in *Coronation Street* when she was 16 and has also acted the parts of hairdresser Debbie Taylor in *Albion Market*, WPC Madeline Forest in *Waterfront Beat*, Lisa Shepherd in *Families* and Joanne Walsh in *Growing Pains*.

As she continues her downward spiral, a more sophisticated-lookingTracy plots revenge on her former pimp, Dez, after his release from prison

'When you hit the front of the car, you are immediately disoriented, but within a split second the windscreen is coming straight at you. I had to teach Thérèse how to become so familiar with the first hit that she could twist immediately to see the windscreen coming at her, then use her hands to bounce off the car and go straight up in the air. She managed the stunt in one take, padded from head to toe.

'We filmed it at night, with headlights on and stuntman James Ryan driving the car. A stunt like this is quite frightening for the driver as well. I told him to go at 30mph without taking his foot off the accelerator. When they went for the take, the sound was so horrendously real that we kept the live sound. Nothing needed to be dubbed. Afterwards, Thérèse just stood up and walked away.'

The murders of Carol's punter Curly, Anita's former lover, George Ferguson, and Tracy's pimp, Dez, made for another whodunit, similar to the first series. This time, however, they were written as a result of Kay's research into the effects of crack cocaine: she was told that users often become paranoid and aggressive, and feel that they want to be violent – or even commit murder. 'So we saw the decline of Tracy, the "sweetie girl" who went for a fiver a time and wouldn't say boo to a goose,' says Kay. 'It's a vicious circle. Prostitutes take crack so that they have the courage to go out on the Lane and do what they do in the first place. Then they use the money they've earned from prostitution to buy more crack. There's nowhere else for them to go but down. That's why I knew I had to tell the truth.'

The shocking ending to the series, in which Tracy, who is revealed to be the murderer, commits suicide, caused Kay a great deal of heartache: 'I would have loved Tracy to kill her father,' she says, 'and that's what everyone probably wanted. But that wouldn't have been truthful. We're talking about a young girl with a history of abuse and crack cocaine. The family wasn't there for her. If she had killed the father, it would have seemed that the problem had gone away. Sadly, problems don't just go away, and that's why we have to be alert to men and women like him who don't take their responsibilities seriously.'

There was another surprise when Carol found herself the beneficiary of Curly's will. Although off the game and in the cleaning business, she still 'walked' for Curly, who was compassionate to her. But the fact that he had left Carol his money and large house incensed Curly's nephew, Vinnie Marshall, who worked in his uncle's chicken factory and had expected to be left everything.

Curly's murder and the almost comic attempt by Carol and Rose to dispose of the body gave Stuart St Paul another stunt to set up. Neither Carol nor Rose could drive, but they put Curly's body in the boot of his car and set off with Carol in the driver's seat. When she failed to change gear, they started kangarooing along the road. They left the handbrake off and got out of the car, which rolled down a hill, smashed into some other cars and then crashed through the window of a sari shop specially built between two houses. 'The residents couldn't believe it when they saw the car come down the hill and smash into it,' says Stuart. 'The problem was that there was a steep drop on the other side of the false shop. Although we put blocks down to help the car to stop, Dave Holland, who was driving it, had to make sure it stopped before he went over the edge. Because the car was supposed to be unoccupied, Dave was lying down in the floorwell, moving the steering wheel without looking. I gave instructions through a walkie-talkie, saying, "Left, left, right, left." Once the car was through the shop window, I yelled "stop".'

One new relationship in the second series was that between Gina's widowed husband, Steve, and her mother, Joyce Webster. They shared a love for the same person and were brought together by grief – although both regretted their one-night stand the morning after. 'For each of them, the relationship was a way of getting back to Gina,' says Kay. 'They were playing mummies and daddies, taking his children to Blackpool and putting them on donkeys. But where does it stop? Do they go to separate bedrooms. Those are difficult areas, and I love difficult areas! That's when it gets interesting.'

The idea of Rose looking for her daughter, Hannah, after giving birth to her at 16 and seeing

Steve and mother-in-law, Joyce, brought together in grief

Rose hired private detective Brian Roberts (Peter Firth) to find her daughter, who was given away for adoption at the age of just two months old

Barbara Dickson
as Anita

After more than 20 years as a successful folk and pop singer, Barbara Dickson emerged as an actress who could play both drama and comedy when she was cast in *Band of Gold* as Anita Braithwaite, former croupier and kept-woman who rents her spare bedroom out to prostitutes. Acting had been her ambition ever since her success a decade before as Mrs Johnston in Willy Russell's *Blood Brothers*, which won her the Society of West End Theatres Award for Best Actress in a Musical.

'I didn't think I could act until I did *Blood Brothers*,' says Barbara. 'When I did it, I just thought: "This is fantastic." I had gone from never acting in my life to doing something very well. Afterwards, when people asked me what was left for me to do, I always said television drama. For 11 years, nobody took me up on it: then I was asked to play two parts – the other was in *Taggart*. I'm very fortunate because it means I can now earn a living either as an actress or as a singer.'

'Casting director Carolyn Bartlett stuck her neck out' says Barbara, 'because there was a lot of resistance to me. I went to a meeting that involved reading a scene from the first episode and it was a complete and utter catastrophe. I left thinking that was the end of it. But, three months later, Richard Standeven, the director, had lunch with me and offered me the role.' Barbara also sang the title song 'Love Hurts' at the end of episodes in the first series.

Meeting prostitutes at the Bradford Working Women's Project drop-in centre helped Barbara to understand their world. 'They spent a lot of time in the pub and many people on the periphery of society came into that pub. My own feeling is that prostitutes simply step over a line to earn a living. There's too much focus on the "dirty deed" rather than on the danger. That's the only reason I'd like prostitution to be legalized.'

After two series of *Band of Gold*, Barbara's next television appearance was as a fisherman's widow in the two-part comedy-drama *The Missing Postman*, starring James Bolam, Alison Steadman and Jim Carter, and directed by Alan Dossor, who had been director of Willy Russell's stage musical *John Paul George Ringo…& Bert* which she also appeared in.

Born in Dunfermline to a Rosyth dockyard worker and his Liverpudlian wife, Barbara originally sang in Scottish folk clubs while working by day as a clerk in the Registrar General's Office, in Edinburgh. She left after four years for a six-week tour of Denmark, and spent the next few years performing on the folk circuit. Then came the opportunity to sing the songs of Lennon and McCartney on stage at the Everyman Theatre, Liverpool, which transferred to London's West End with a cast that included actors Bernard Hill, Trevor Eve and George Costigan.

Then came a recording contract and pop hits such as 'Answer Me', 'Another Suitcase in Another Hall', 'Caravan Song' and 'January February', before she starred in the West End musical *Blood Brothers*. But by the time she had a No. 1 single in 1985 with 'I Know Him So Well' – a duet from the musical *Chess*, performed with Elaine Paige – Barbara had begun to move away from mainstream pop.

'When I made my last pop album, *Coming Alive Again*, in 1989, I said: "I shouldn't be making music like this – it's nothing to do with what I want to do." ' Her 1994 album, *Parcel of Rogues*, was a collection of traditional songs from around the British isles.

Then came the chance to act in television drama. Scottish Television cast her in the *Taggart* story 'Legends' as a former pop star. It was screened after *Band of Gold*. Barbara has also been planning a stage project, *Seven Ages of Woman*, with theatre producer Chris Bond, who directed *Blood Brothers*.

Married to freelance television production manager Oliver Cookson, with three sons – Colm, Gabriel and Archie – Barbara lives in Lincolnshire.

her taken away for adoption within two months, came from a story told to Kay by Trea, the prostitute on whom Carol was based. 'Trea said that one of her friends who married a punter had given a kid up for adoption years earlier,' recalls Kay. 'One day, as a result of the new laws allowing people to trace their real parents, this kid knocked on her door and said, "I'm your daughter." She, too, was a prostitute, which prompts so many questions. Is it nature or nurture? She hadn't even brought her daughter up. But I think that it's what a woman falls back on, if she gets down low enough. And it wasn't necessarily a coincidence, because Trea's friend must have reached a low point in her life when she gave her daughter up. The daughter, too, was probably brought up in care or might have been abused.'

In the programme, Rose decides to hire a private detective, Brian Roberts, to track down Hannah. And after finding Hannah's adoptive sister and mother, Rose discovers that Hannah ended up in a children's home when she was 12 – and later hears the shocking news that Colette is her daughter. The final episode ended with Rose

Tracy, whose tragic decline through increasing drug addiction was witnessed during the second series, fell for bondage prostitute Colette, and even tried out the equipment in her dungeon

Curly's chicken factory was seen for the first time when Carol paid her sugar daddy a surprise visit

no Yorkshire hills in the background, as in the previous series.

'Gina was no longer with us, having died, although we did have an interior of her house at Spectrum Arena for scenes with her husband, Steve, his mother-in-law, Joyce, and girlfriend Lisa. Joyce still had her location in Stalybridge, and an interior set in the studio.'

The development of characters was reflected in some of Chris's sets. Carol's living room, filmed on a set at Spectrum, was redecorated with floral wallpaper to help to create a family environment in which Emma could grow up, as Carol's punter, Curly, showed more interest in Carol and her daughter's welfare. Also, Anita lived with Carol during the second series, having been thrown out of her flat in the first one.

For the first time, Rose was seen in her own, rented house, which she shared with Tracy, whose friend Colette eventually moved in, bringing clients back and using the cellar when the punters asked for sadomasochistic sex. Its exteriors were shot on location in Ashton-under-Lyne, where Chris found an almost derelict house close to the pub that was used as the Hustler's Arms. Its interiors were filmed on sets at Spectrum: there was a ground-floor set, comprising living room, dining room and kitchen; a first-floor set, comprising two bedrooms; and a separate cellar set. Chris gave the interior a gloomy, rundown feel to establish its seedy setting, but added a few expensive items, such as a hi-fi and light fittings, which Colette and Tracy would have bought with their earnings from prostitution.

'The cellar in which Colette saw her sado-masochistic punters involved a lot of props,' says Chris. 'But Elizabeth Bradley, the producer, met a specialist in London and passed the necessary information on to me. Then Ron Pritchard, my props buyer, went off to Manchester sex shops and bought handcuffs, whips, leather thongs and masks.'

When Rose travelled to Manchester in pursuit of the young woman she believed to be her

and Colette leaving the Hustler's Arms in freeze frame: viewers could only guess whether Rose was about to confront Colette with the truth.

Once the storylines had been hammered out, and the characters had been developed further, the team faced the challenges of a new production. Six months after the first series ended, the real-life problems in Bradford meant that the police advised Granada Television not to film the second series there, but this did not create any major problems for production designer Chris Wilkinson. 'All we had to do was find another school for Carol's daughter, Emma,' he says. 'We found one in Ashton-under-Lyne, where we shot more of our street scenes this time. It was built of stone, so it could have been in Yorkshire, but it didn't have a huge playground and there were

Gold

Rose Garrity is determined to make a go of Scrubbit's cleaning contract at the council leisure centre. She is now sharing a house with Tracy, whose new friend, Colette, she hates. Rose sets about finding her long-lost daughter, Hannah, who was taken away from her shortly after birth.

Carol Johnson is determined to stay off the game after joining the Scrubbit cleaning co-operative, but soon tires of getting out of bed early and covering for colleagues. She has not 'walked' for Curly for months; he is keen for her to do so and tells her that he is changing his will in her favour.

Anita Braithwaite now lives with Carol and is the key to ex-lover George Ferguson's attempts to launder money through Scrubbit. She sees through George, double-crosses him and pays the price.

Tracy Richards is sharing a house with Rose but threatening their friendship by becoming closer to bondage prostitute Colette, who introduces her to crack cocaine. She is on a downhill slope as the drugs combine with the effects of her father's sexual abuse, which she is still haunted by.

Colette is a leather-clad bondage prostitute who becomes Tracy's friend, which makes her the arch enemy of Rose. She leads Tracy on a downward spiral of drug abuse and becomes her lesbian lover.

Joyce Webster is coming to terms with the death of her daughter, Gina, as she manages Scrubbit. She gets closer to son-in-law Steve when she takes her grandchildren to see him in Blackpool, where he is working.

daughter, who was given up for adoption as a baby, she was seen pretending to be interested in buying an instrument in a music shop in the All Saints area of the city called Johnny Roadhouse, where Sarah worked. Both outside and inside were used for filming. Then another house in Didsbury was used when Rose went to meet Sarah at home, and listened to her playing the cello.

The film crew went to Blackpool to shoot scenes of Joyce visiting her son-in-law, Steve, with whom she was having an affair. 'We filmed in the front room of a boarding house on the front so that

we could see all the illuminations outside,' says Chris, 'but we went to Spectrum to shoot the scenes of Joyce and Steve making love in the guest-house bedroom, with quite an elaborate scenic backing with illuminations on it.'

Other new locations in the second series included Curly's house and chicken factory. 'The problem I had,' recalls Chris, 'is that there are no chicken factories in which chickens are processed from start to finish in the Manchester area. But Curly bred chickens, then killed, processed and packaged them. The nearest factory like Curly's that we could find was in Carlisle, so we sent a second unit there to shoot some interior scenes of chickens being processed. Then we shot the exterior of the factory at a unit on a trading estate in Hyde, Cheshire – I had a larger-than-life caricature of Curly holding a chicken made, which we put up outside the unit!

'Because of the constraints of filming, we had to ensure that some of locations were reasonably near to each other, so we looked for Curly's house near Buxton, where we were shooting the exterior of Tracy's parents' home. We discussed at length what type of house Curly would have owned, and eventually decided that it would be large, and we discovered a large imposing house built of

Georgian stone, called Aspenshaw Hall, and shot the exteriors there.'

It was not practical for the film crew to travel all the way to Harrogate to shoot just one exterior of Tracy's parents' house for the final episode, so Chris had to find a house closer to Manchester that matched the Harrogate house he had used in the first series. He came up with the aforementioned one in Buxton, Derbyshire, which fitted the bill for exterior shots; and one in Didsbury, Manchester, for interiors. 'The Buxton street was similar to the one we had used in Harrogate,' says Chris, 'and I just had to change the front door of the house. Then we had to find a location closer to base, because a couple of days were needed for

Trying to stay off the streets by running Scrubbit is the task facing Carol, Joyce, Anita and Rose, but George Ferguson is a perennial threat to their cleaning business

Rose hopes that a meeting with private detective Brian Roberts in the Hustler's Arms will lead to the discovery of her daughter, whom she gave away for adoption as a baby

filming the interior scenes, which we eventually found in Didsbury.'

By the time the series went out – complete with drugs, bondage and chicken factory – Gub Neal had taken over as Granada Television's controller of drama, and Sally Head had assumed the same role at LWT, following Granada's purchase of the company. Once more, *Band of Gold* was a hit with viewers – and this time it won the Television and Radio Industries Club ITV Programme of the Year award.

SERIES TWO: THE STORY

Episode One: Hustling

As tracy teams up with bondage specialist Colette, George Ferguson leaves prison after his sentence for fraud and tells drug baron Alf that he can launder money through the Scrubbit cleaning co-operative. Curly informs Carol that he is changing his will in her favour and wants her to 'walk' for him again. Meanwhile, George goes to extreme measures to get his revenge after Anita double-crosses him.

Tracy Richards is lying naked on a bed with a punter, having had sex, in a Bradford hotel room. She lifts his arm off her carefully and starts to get out of bed: 'Where do you think you're going?' he asks, grabbing her shoulder. 'I paid for a night with you and I want a whole night, not part of a night.' The repugnant man then ties Tracy's hands to the bed and approaches her with a large roll of sticky tape.

Meanwhile, George Ferguson steps out of Wakefield Prison – he is on parole after serving his sentence for fraud. A car pulls up alongside him, and Smiley, the driver, asks if he would like a lift. George gets in the back, where big-time gangster and drug-dealer Alf is on his mobile phone. Once the call is over, Alf tells George: 'You owe me 200 grand, sunshine.'

Tracy's friend Colette, dressed in tight black leather trousers and vest, a chunky belt and black, pointed high boots with buckles and studs, arrives at the hotel room as Tracy struggles to get free. Colette knocks at the door, but there is no reply so she turns to leave. Unable to shout through the gag of sticky-tape, Tracy uses her head to knock a telephone off the bedside cabinet. Colette gets a pass key from a cleaner and rushes in to rescue her.

When Alf asks him about the money, George claims he invested it in a loan company. 'If I'd have wanted a shark I'd have gone to the Atlantic,' Alf replies. 'I came to you 'cause you were a small fish – a small, clean fish – and you know what happens to small fish when they try swimming against the tide: they get hooked up, battered and served up on someone else's plate.' George claims that his wife, Kathleen, took all his money. When Alf puts the pressure on, George suggests that he could launder money through 'this other cleaning company' – meaning the one set up by the former prostitutes.

Joyce Webster, Rose Garrity and Carol Johnson visit leisure centre manager Mrs Minkin, who tells them that she is to become general manager for civic health and leisure, and there is an opportunity for them to be awarded the health centre contract. Meanwhile, back at Rose's house, Tracy and Colette sit in the living room smoking crack from a home-made pipe, while George pulls up alongside Anita in his Jaguar as she takes Emma to school for Carol, who has left home early for her cleaning job. George wheedles his way back into Anita's affections, telling her he has been thinking about her and is no longer with the woman for whom he dumped her.

At lunchtime, Rose meets private detective Brian Roberts, whom she has hired to track down her daughter, Hannah, who was adopted as a baby. Back at her house Anita knocks on the front door as Tracy and Colette are lying on the sofa in the living room after finishing the rock. When Tracy lets her in, Anita says she is looking for Rose. Tracy says she is not there but asks Anita to be her maid for £6 an hour, letting punters in, taking their money and keeping an eye on her.

In his office at Durkin's Chickens factory, Curly is asked by his nephew, Vinnie Marshall, when he is planning to retire. But 'Uncle Granville' tells him he will discuss his plans the following day. Then Vinnie joins his classy fiancée Claudia in her car as Curly arrives at Carol's house with an Indian takeaway. He hands Emma a bar of chocolate, and she thanks her 'Uncle Granville'.

George takes Anita, dressed in a shocking pink suit with lipstick and nail varnish to match, to his club. He explains that the fact that his wife Kathleen's money is in Scrubbit, the women's cleaning co-operative, means that – considering his impending divorce – he owns half of it. When Rose berates Tracy for mixing with Colette, Tracy says that Colette has been in children's homes from the age of seven. Rose tells Tracy that she is trying to find her daughter, Hannah, who was taken away from her at the age of two months. Put out by this news, Tracy leaves the house.

Curly tells Carol he will pay her £200 a week – an increase of £50 – if she wants to give up her job as a cleaner. He also says that he is planning to change his will in her favour. But when Curly asks Carol to 'walk' for him for the first time in months, she tells him: 'Either I "walk" for you or I'm your friend.'

Over dinner, George tells Anita that he believes she has a brain but has never had the chance to use it. This wins her round – but she does not know his real intentions. When George drives her back to Rose's house, she is disappointed that he does not want to sleep with her. After a long kiss, he tells her to ring him at his office when she has decided what she wants to do about his proposal that she be a manager of Klenzit and that he invest money in Scrubbit. Anita then walks in on Carol 'walking' for Curly. Later, in the kitchen, Carol berates Anita for getting Emma to school late and Anita tells her about George's proposal. In the Lane, Anita tells Rose about George wanting to put money into Scrubbit.

At Joyce's house, her three grandchildren talk to their father, Steve Dixon, who is on a pay phone in a guest-house in Blackpool, where he is working. Steve asks Joyce whether she can bring the children there for a visit. As Joyce winds up the phone call, Rose, Carol and Anita arrive and tell her about George, whom Joyce blames for Gina's death. 'He's changed,' Anita insists, adding that he owns part of Scrubbit. Joyce tells Anita to leave her house.

Back at Rose's house, Anita takes a phone call for Tracy from a punter and makes an appointment. At the same time, Colette arrives, saying that Lionel, a client, is outside in a car, but that she cannot get a hotel room because of a convention taking place. When she brings Lionel in and whips him, Anita joins in, booting him in the backside. Later, he reappears as a respectable businessman – a corporate solicitor – and tells Anita to beware of her friend George.

Later, Anita goes to the Hustler's Arms, where Rose, Carol and Joyce are already drinking. After Rose breaks the news that they have landed the health centre contract, Anita admits that the others were right about George and apologizes to Joyce. Then, planning to set George up, she visits him at his Klenzit offices and tells him that 'they're on for it'. George sets off immediately for the Town Hall, where the Scrubbit women are waiting to see him. As he arrives, he calls Alf on his mobile phone: 'We should be in business by the end of the week,' he tells the drugs baron, who is hosting a party at his penthouse apartment. As Alf finishes the call, Tracy – high on drugs – walks up to him and dances provocatively.

At the Town Hall, George walks into the conference room, where the women are sitting at a table. He says that he can offer their new company

Anita visits George at his Klenzit offices and tells him that the Scrubbit women 'are on for it'

capital, as well as advice based on over 20 years' experience in the cleaning business. Rose tells George that they now have both health centre contracts, and they might win a library contract as well. She then asks what the council would think about him investing in their business, in view of the fact that he had been sent to prison for corruption. Anita says that what George told her about owning part of Scrubbit was 'complete and utter rubbish', adding that any investment money could be 'dodgy'. After he tells the women that he has money deposited in off-shore accounts, Anita pulls out a cassette-recorder, plays the confession back to him and threatens to take the tape to the police if he 'pulls a fast one' on her again. 'I'll see you in Hell,' he says, before storming out of the room.

Afterwards, the women have a drink in the Hustler's Arms. Anita lets slip that Colette had taken a client back to Rose's house. Rose is furious and storms out, and, as she does so, Carol tells Anita that she hates Colette. Anita remembers that she had agreed to go to a party with Tracy, and rushes out of the pub. George, waiting in his Jaguar, drives straight at her: she is thrown on to the bonnet and falls, face down, on the road. George picks her handbag up off the ground and drives away.

Episode Two: Kiss

Joyce takes her grandchildren to Blackpool to visit Steve. Rose covers her cleaning shift after Carol refuses to do so; she is looking after Emma in Anita's absence – she is in hospital after the hit-and-run incident. George tips off a newspaper that the council is employing prostitutes to clean the leisure centre. After Curly tells his nephew Vinnie that he isn't going to retire and hand over the chicken factory to him, Carol finds Curly dead.

An angry Rose wakes Tracy, who is asleep on the sofa in her party dress, and tells her that she will give her 'the biggest, good hidin' you've ever had' if she lets Colette use her bedroom again. As Tracy is insisting that Colette did not use Rose's bedroom, the phone rings: Carol is calling to say that she cannot do her cleaning shift because Anita is not at her house to look after Emma, who has a day off school. Rose, exasperated, says that she must go to the leisure centre, but Carol points out that she is simply covering for Joyce, who is taking her grandchildren to Blackpool to see their father, and that there is no one to cover for her. Carol slams down the phone, saying she will not do it. Rose, infuriated, does the cleaning shift herself.

Meanwhile, George phones the *Daily News* and tells a reporter that at least two of the women who run Scrubbit are 'known prostitutes' and now work at the council's leisure centre and both health centres. Carol takes Emma to Curly's chicken factory and is awe-struck when she sees a vast modern building with a large sign that reads 'Durkin's Chickens' and carries a caricature of Curly. Once they are inside, Curly introduces Carol to his office manager, June, and shows Carol and Emma round the factory.

Back at Rose's house, Colette throws stones up at Tracy's window because one of her punters is sitting outside in his car. Tracy lets Colette in, but tells her that she cannot use the house again because Rose found out about her previous client. 'I just want you out,' she says. Colette claims that Rose is turning Tracy against her, but Tracy explains that she is just 'on a bit of a downer'.

Mrs Minkin approaches Rose at the leisure centre, and tells her that a newspaper reporter has been asking the council about allegations that two of the women have criminal records for prostitution. Later, Rose tells Carol that she told the truth to Mrs Minkin, and that she had pledged to stand by Scrubbit.

Joyce and her three grandchildren, Sarah, Michelle and Joanne, travel to Blackpool by coach to meet Steve, who greets Joanne as 'birthday girl'. Back in Bradford, Carol arrives home and is approached by DC Barstow, who asks whether

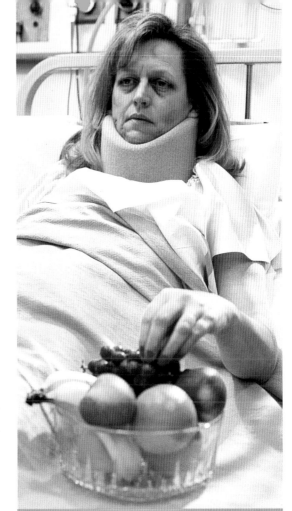

Anita is left in hospital with her neck in a brace after George runs her over in his Jaguar

Anita lives with her. As Rose arrives, she sees Carol leaving in the back of a police car. Carol is taken to the hospital, where Anita is conscious and sitting up in bed wearing a neck brace.

Brenda Taylor, one of George's former employees who now works for Scrubbit, visits George at his Klenzit office and asks for her job back, because it would give her an opportunity to earn money 'cash in hand'. He refuses, saying that she had been disloyal, and tells her to close the door behind her. However, when a *Daily News* reporter telephones George claiming not to be able to 'stand up' the story about convicted prostitutes working at the leisure centre, George slams the phone down and decides to visit Brenda. Apologizing for being so hasty earlier, George –

SAMANTHA MORTON
AS TRACY

The haunting memory of 'sweetie girl' Tracy, spotted plying her trade in Bradford's red-light district by writer Kay Mellor, was brought to the screen in an intense performance by teenage actress Samantha Morton.

On screen, Tracy Richards was a 15-year-old runaway who had left her respectable, middle-class parents' home in Harrogate after being sexually abused by her father. In Bradford, Tracy was spotted by a pimp, Dez Sadiq, who befriended her, put her on the game and made her reliant on drugs. Off screen, Nottingham-born Samantha's parents split up when she was three,

and, after living with her father and stepmother for the next six years, she was taken into local-authority care. Growing up with foster families and in five different children's homes, she lived among girls who had become prostitutes at an early age.

'A lot of the girls who came into the community home I was in were prostitutes by the time they were 14,' revealed Samantha. 'but I was determined it was never going to happen to me. Many got into it through their boyfriends or their mothers – or because they wanted to be grown-up.'

Samantha's escape came with her dream of acting. She auditioned at the Theatre Royal, Nottingham, from the age of 10, and wrote to television companies complaining that their actors were awful and stating that she could do better. Eventually, Samantha's nearest ITV company, Central Television, invited her to join its Junior Television Workshop when she was 13.

She made her screen début in the schools programme *Talk Write and Read*, before landing small roles in *Soldier Soldier* and *Boon*, and presenting two series of the children's show *Go Wild*. Samantha

also appeared in *Peak Practice* before first getting noticed as a schoolgirl having an affair with her headmaster in *Cracker*. By the time *Cracker* was screened, Samantha – then just 17 – had been chosen for the role of Tracy in *Band of Gold*, after leaving the original producer, Tony Dennis, and director, Richard Standeven, open-mouthed with stories of her childhood.

'I've met girls like Tracy and I get angry because they have no choice,' said Samantha. 'They are too young to claim benefits, they're worried about going into care and many can't go home because of sexual abuse. In Tracy's mind, the only option open to her is to control her own life and earn money through sex.'

When Tracy was first seen on the Lane, Rose, resenting the appearance of ever younger prostitutes, told her to 'go play with yer Wendy house'. But after the murder of Gina Dixon, Rose took Tracy under her wing. Later Tracy accompanied Rose to London, where she became more sophisticated, spending her money on expensive clothes and make-up.

In the second series, Tracy was back in Bradford, where she teamed up with crack-smoking bondage prostitute Colette. Increasingly reliant on the drug, and driven to violence by it, Tracy left three men dead with slit throats. The tragic ending to the series saw Tracy return to her parents' home, where her father – the source of her problems – insisted on looking through family photograph albums. Afterwards, she went to her bedroom and slashed her wrist.

Since *Band of Gold*, Samantha has been much in demand. She has starred alongside Richard Harris, John Lynch and Gabriel Byrne in *This Is the Sea*, and acted in the British Film Institute production *Under the Skin*. On television, she played a schoolgirl seductress in *The Vet*, a dying AIDS victim in *Medics*, Harriet Smith in Andrew Davies's adaptation of Jane Austen's *Emma* and the title role in *Jane Eyre*, adapted by Kay Mellor, before starring in a BBC production of Henry Fielding's *Tom Jones*.

trying to get Brenda to pass on incriminating information – explains that he had earmarked her as the person to take over from Joyce as the cleaners' manageress, and points out that he has lost the contract for the leisure centre contract, and possibly the contracts for the health centres, too.

At the Hustler's Arms, Tracy is with Colette, who uses her mobile phone to call Rabbit, who supplies her with drugs. Standing in the Lane, he tells her that he believes he is being watched by undercover police officers. Shortly afterwards, Rabbit walks into the pub and puts

When Rose threatens to leave, Tracy panics and tells her: 'If you go, I'll kill myself'

a packet containing one-sixteenth of an ounce of crack in the ashtray on the table in front of Colette. Tracy and Colette take it into a toilet cubicle and smoke the rock. Later, Tracy returns home to be told by Rose that she does not want any more punters in the house, or any 'used rubbers floating down the pot'. When Rose threatens to leave, Tracy panics and tells her: 'If you go, I'll kill myself…You're the only good thing in my life.' Rose holds Tracy close, but is shocked when Tracy tries to kiss her. She tells Tracy that she loves her 'like family', not in the way her father loved her. 'What he did was nothin' to do wi' love,' Rose adds.

In the hospital, Sister Stanley tells Anita that her brother phoned earlier enquiring after her. After a few seconds' thought, Anita – who does not have a brother – mutters: 'George.' At Durkin's Chickens factory, Curly tells his nephew, Vinnie, that he has had second thoughts about taking early retirement the following year and is thinking of 'settling down'. Vinnie storms out. Meanwhile, private detective Brian Roberts tells Rose in the Hustler's Arms that he believes he is close to tracking down her daughter. A contact in social services has told him that Hannah had gone to live with foster parents and that later they applied to adopt her.

Back at the chicken factory, Vinnie questions June, the office manager, about Carol. When she

leaves, Vinnie looks in his uncle's address book and drives to Carol's house, where he looks in through the window and sees Carol 'walking' for Curly. Later, Rose arrives at the house, walks in and finds Carol scrubbing away at the carpet. Curly is sitting in the chair: his throat has been cut and there is blood everywhere. Rose exclaims: 'What the hell have you done?' Carol says that they cannot call the police because they will think that she murdered Curly. Then, wondering aloud whether she could have killed him herself, Carol says: 'Tell me I haven't done it.' Suddenly, Emma walks into the house with baby-sitter Julie. In a panic, Carol gives them money to go to the cinema. Once they have gone, Rose tells Carol that they must use Curly's car to dump his body. She then sets about putting him in a black bin bag.

At the leisure centre, Brenda tells Mrs Minkin that Carol often cleaned the sauna and steam room while leaving her to handle the changing room and toilets. She adds that another cleaner had seen Carol in the sauna with a man who gave her money. Mrs Minkin calls in George to ask him about Brenda, since she is an ex-employee of his. He says that Brenda is a gossip – but that she is honest.

After a day on the beach at Blackpool, Steve and Joyce return to his guest-house. They tuck the children into bed and then sit in Steve's room drinking cans of beer. Feeling young and relaxed, Joyce says that she has had a wonderful day. 'Aye, so have I,' says Steve – before they kiss one another and fall back on the bed.

Rose and Carol carry Curly's body out to his car, but they set off the alarm when they try to unlock the boot – but after pressing the key to stop the alarm, they manage to lift their heavy load into it. Then the pair realize that neither of them can drive. So, with Carol in the driver's seat, they set off along the street, kangarooing because she cannot change gear properly. Eventually, they get out of

The blood-drenched body of Curly in Carol's home starts a new series of murders and puts
Carol under suspicion following Curly's decision to change his will in her favour

Curly is besotted with Carol and still pays her to 'walk' for him. But he reveals himself to be Granville Durkin, the wealthy owner of a chicken factory, and promises to leave Carol his fortune and his large house in his will. Nephew Vinnie Marshall, who works for him, is furious when he hears about his uncle's decision to change his will in Carol's favour.

Dez Sadiq is Tracy's pimp, who hit her over the head and left her for dead.

Eventually he is released from jail. He is keen to 'look after' Tracy again, as well as her friend, Colette, but Tracy has not forgotten what he did to her.

George Ferguson is out on parole after being jailed for fraud, and he has to find money for drugs baron Alf. His plan to launder money through Scrubbit goes wrong and former lover Anita betrays him. In revenge he wins back the leisure centre cleaning contract.

the car, but forget to put the handbrake on: the car starts to roll down the hill, knocks into other vehicles and ends up crashing into the front of a sari shop. Rose and Carol run away.

Episode Three: Betrayal

As Joyce leaves Blackpool with her grandchildren, Mrs Minkin confronts Rose with the newspaper story about prostitutes being employed by the council to clean the leisure centre. Rose walks out on Tracy after finding her in bed with Colette, and Carol is questioned about Curly's murder and locked up in a police cell. George sets up a new company to launder money for drugs baron Alf, has his car's headlights smashed by Anita and ends up with his throat slit.

In Bradford Tracy and Colette lie in bed in each other's arms, while Joyce quietly steps out of Steve's single bed in Blackpool and leaves his room, feeling guilty about having slept with her son-in-law. Later, he enters the attic room in which Joyce is getting her grandchildren ready for their journey home, and she remarks that Steve has shaved off his moustache: 'I were sick of it,' he

replies. Steve drives them all to the coach station and promises to phone the children that evening.

As Rose sets off for the leisure centre to cover for Joyce and Carol, she sees a police recovery vehicle carrying Curly's car away. When she arrives at the centre, she sees Mrs Minkin with George. Mrs Minkin then presents Rose with a newspaper whose front-page story claims the cleaners have been using the leisure centre for prostitution. Rose then tells her to 'stick yer bleedin' contract up yer arse'.

At Durkin's Chickens factory, DC Barstow informs the office manager, June, and Curly's nephew, Vinnie, that Curly is dead. Meanwhile, Rose finds Colette in bed with Tracy. And, after an argument, Rose packs her case and says that she is moving out. She bumps into Carol in the road, and the pair see police cars parked outside Carol's house. DCI Newall gets out of his car as Carol approaches her house: 'Your sugar daddy's been murdered and your fingerprints are all over his car,' he tells her.

At Turton Lane Police Station, Newall and DS Hoyle ask Carol about her relationship with Curly. She explains that she 'walked' for him, adding that she is 'hardly likely to slit his throat', which gives her away. 'And how did you know that his throat had been cut?' asks Newall, who instructs Hoyle to arrange for a forensic team to go through Carol's house.

After Rose tells Joyce about losing the cleaning contract, Joyce confronts Mrs Minkin in her office at the leisure centre but is told that the council has made its decision. Joyce says that George's company, Klenzit, will get the contract 'over my dead body' and storms out.

As Rose walks towards Carol's house, suitcase in hand, she is stopped by private detective Brian Roberts. He offers her a lift and hands her a piece of paper as she gets into the passenger seat. 'What's this?' she asks. 'Name and address of where yer daughter is,' he replies. At the Hustler's Arms, 'sweetie girl' Tula approaches drug dealer Rabbit as Rose discusses with Brian how she will approach her daughter, whom he has tracked down to Manchester. But, as they speak, Tracy walks in and Rose is shocked to see her sit down with Rabbit: 'He's a crack-head, Tracy,' Rose tells her. Rabbit grabs Rose, but Brian pulls him off her, and Rose and Brian leave.

When Tracy leaves the pub, she runs down the street after Rabbit, knowing that he fancies her. She asks him to give her some drugs and 'put it on the slate' – he grabs Tracy, stands her against a wall, kisses her and gives her £60 worth of drugs.

Back at the police station, Carol confesses that she found Curly dead in her armchair on returning from a visit to Anita in hospital. Newall puts a box containing an expensive solitaire diamond ring on the table in front of Carol. As the interview continues, he tells Carol to take the ring out of the box – it was found in Curly's jacket pocket. She does so and reads the inscription: 'Carol and Granville'.

Tracy arrives at the hospital with flowers for Anita and asks: 'What's up wi' yer?' Anita replies, 'What's up with me? I'll tell yer what. I've been concussed for 13 hours, I've got internal bruising, suspected cracked ribs and I feel as if I've done three

Mrs Minkin confronts Rose with allegations about Scrubbit, fed to a newspaper reporter by George

rounds with Mike Tyson.' Anita shows Tracy the newspaper story that has lost Scrubbit the cleaning contract, and tells her that George must have been responsible for it – and also for running her over. And as Tracy leaves the ward, she remembers lying in bed in another of the hospital's wards, after being hit on the head by her pimp, Dez. She imagines that she can see Dez, dressed as a doctor, coming down the corridor towards her.

At the chicken factory, office manager June shows Vinnie a file containing his uncle's will, which leaves everything to Carol. As Vinnie storms out of the office, June telephones the police and tells DC Barstow about it. Armed with this information, Newall returns to the interview room to confront Carol: 'You killed him for the money,' he tells her. This comes as news to Carol and she cries, saying she is doing so because Curly was 'a stupid, soft bastard'. Newall tries to kiss her passionately, but she resists. Just for a moment, Carol stops resisting – revealing that she feels something for him – then breaks the kiss and spits in his face. 'I friggin' hate yer,' she screams. Then, Newall orders Carol to be locked up in a cell. Vinnie turns up at Carol's house, looking for her, but Rose tells her that she is not there. 'Tell her I saw her,' he says as he leaves.

> *Carol stops resisting – revealing that she feels something for him – then breaks the kiss and spits in his face*

When Joyce turns up at Brenda's house, Brenda presumes that she has found out about what she had told Mrs Minkin. In fact, Joyce asks her to look after her grandchildren for an hour. Then Brenda receives a telephone call from George, telling her that the job they had discussed didn't work out, but explaining that he has won back the leisure centre cleaning contract and can offer her a cash-in-hand job, if she will agree to 'sign a few cheques and papers for me'. She accepts this and George telephones Alf with the news that he will have a new company set up within a week, fronted by Brenda Taylor.

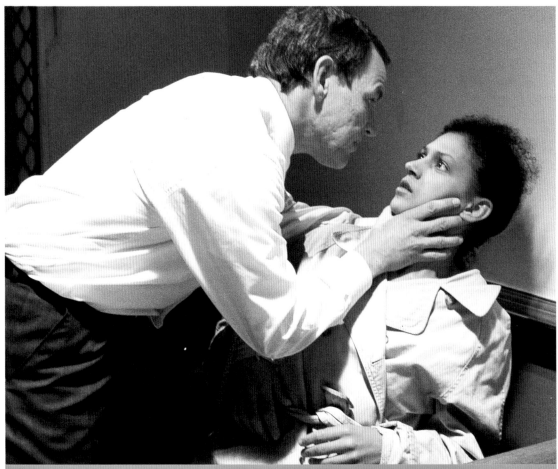

The intensity of their long-running relationship bubbles over as DCI Newall interrogates Carol about Curly's murder and is surprised to discover that she did not know about his will or the ring in his jacket pocket

Anita – who has discharged herself from hospital – hobbles up to George's Jaguar in the Klenzit car park and smashes the headlights with one of her crutches. Meanwhile, Alf puts his mobile phone down and talks to Tracy, who is alongside him in the back of his car. She tells him that she wants the crack that he has given her to be washed, and he calls her a 'little crackhead'. As he tries to pull Tracy towards him, she screams: 'Don't touch me!' At that, Alf orders chauffeur Smiley to stop the car and tells Tracy: 'Now get yer pretty little face and yer arse out of my car.'

Leaving his office, George sets off for the car park and takes a call on his mobile phone. 'There's nothing you can tell me about Scrubbit that I don't already know,' he says 'And I'm on my way home… Really, now you've got me guessing…I'll be there in a minute.' As George walks into the car park, a knife appears out of the darkness and slits his throat. He slumps to the ground in front of his Jaguar, screaming for help, as blood pours from him.

Episode Four. Hurt

Carol is released after George Ferguson's dead body is discovered and Joyce is taken in for questioning. Colette fits out her bondage dungeon and Rose goes in search of her daughter. Alf asks Tracy to make a drugs run for him, but she is arrested by police after young prostitute Tula tips them off. Tracy claims that Colette is her supplier.

Tracy's state of mind is such that she is even prepared to shop her best friend

DCI Newall and DS Hoyle leave the scene of George Ferguson's murder as the forensic technicians get to work. He orders Carol to be released on bail: 'Did you see the man's throat? That wasn't planned. That was somebody who's sick up here, somebody who kills just for the hell of it. It wasn't Carol Johnson. We've got the wrong person locked up.'

As Carol walks home, Newall pulls up alongside and tells her that George has been murdered. 'God knows where yer gonna start looking for this one 'cause everybody wanted that bastard dead,' says Carol. Newall drives her home, and follows her in for a 'freebie'. He starts kissing Carol in the

hallway as Anita walks down the stairs looking rough and asks if she has any painkillers. She is shocked to hear of George's death, and admits to smashing his car headlights.

In the cellar of Tracy and Colette's house, a carpenter has fastened two vertical strips of wood to the wall, each with a manacle attached at shoulder height: it is the first step in fitting out Colette's bondage dungeon. But as the carpenter is leaving, Colette receives a call from a client. She immediately calls him back and asks him to erect a cross. Then Tracy practises using one of Colette's whips. 'More it hurts, more they like it,' explains Colette.

'Sometimes, they're red raw and I'm knackered by the time they're done.'

Tracy asks how the manacles work and pleads with Colette to treat her in the same way as one of her punters: 'I want you to hurt me,' says Tracy. 'I want you to stop me brain from thinkin'. I want you to make me feel better.' Colette refuses, and Tracy tries to kiss her. 'I can't do it,' says Colette. 'I could never bloody hate you.' Before she storms out, Tracy replies: 'You will, though. I'll make sure of that!' Outside, Smiley tells Tracy that Alf wants to see her and she gets into his Rolls-Royce.

At the police station, Anita explains to Newall that she smashed the headlights of George's Jaguar in revenge for everything he had done to her, as well as for shopping Scrubbit to the newspapers. Back at Carol's house, Carol receives a call from Vinnie: 'I saw you with my uncle,' he tells her. 'I want you to know that you're not gettin' a penny of his money, not one.'

Rose goes to Manchester in pursuit of her daughter and sees a young woman leaving the address that Brian gave her. Rose then follows her to the music shop in which she works. To make conversation, Rose tells the young woman that she is looking for a musical instrument for her daughter. Later, Rose contrives to bump into her in a park. The young woman says that she is selling her cello privately, and that if Rose would like to buy it, she is happy to take her home for her to have a look at it. She then tells Rose that her name is Sarah Levison.

Back in Bradford, Alf is having sex with Tracy at his penthouse. 'Yer takin' yer time,' she tells Alf, who explains that a big business deal is putting him under a great deal of stress. Alf rolls off Tracy, who masturbates him as he asks her to pick up a package in Belgium: 'There'll be a couple of grams on account,' he adds.

Carol panics, discovers Emma is not in her bedroom and hears the telephone ring. 'Mum!' Emma shouts

Steve returns from Blackpool with Lisa and her young son from the guest-house and tells Joyce that his job there has finished. But when Steve asks if Lisa and the boy can stay with her, she refuses. Then there is a knock at the door: it is DC Barstow, who announces that he is arresting Joyce on suspicion of murdering George Ferguson. At the police station, Newall tells Joyce that George had robbed her of both her daughter and her cleaning business, and says that he can understand her bitterness. Joyce cannot provide an alibi for the time of George's death, simply saying that she was visiting Gina's grave in the dark. 'I had to make my peace with her,' says Joyce, who admits to having had a one-night stand with Gina's husband, Steve, and feels that she has betrayed her daughter: 'I needed her to forgive me.' Steve is waiting inside the station to take Joyce home when she is released.

In the Hustler's Arms, young prostitute Tula tells Tracy that her pimp, Dez, is due to be released. Rabbit walks over and, after Tula leaves, is shocked to see the size of the large rock of crack that Alf has given Tracy. From a car outside, Tula points Tracy out to DC Gregson, who gives her £50, before following Tracy and Rabbit to Rabbit's house.

Carol's daughter, Emma, leaves home to go swimming with her friend Melanie, telling Carol that Melanie's mother will bring her home later. Meanwhile, Vinnie talks to his uncle's solicitor, who explains that Curly wanted £20,000 to be left to Emma and the rest of his estate – valued at £4.5 million – to Carol, so long as she survives his death by at least 30 days. If Carol were to die within that period, the money would go to Vinnie.

Later, Vinnie arrives at Carol's house. Rose lies to him, saying that Carol is not there. 'My boyfriend's upstairs tryin' to sleep and if yer wake him he'll kick yer head in,' she shouts. But as he turns round to leave, Emma is dropped off by her friend's mother. Seizing his chance, Vinnie tells Emma that Carol is at the police station and he has been sent to pick her up.

Ten minutes later, Carol arrives at Mrs Clark's house, looking for Emma. Told that she had already been brought home, Carol panics, runs back to her house, discovers Emma is not in her bedroom and hears the telephone ring. Vinnie, with Emma in his car, holds his mobile phone to her ear. 'Mum!' she shouts, as a near-hysterical Carol answers her telephone. Vinnie, not noticing Newall pulling up at the same junction, tells Carol to meet him near the canal if he wants to see Emma again. The girl waves to Newall in his car, but he is oblivious to what is happening. Carol is frantic when he arrives on her doorstep.

At the police station, an agitated Tracy – who is desperate for some crack – is being interrogated by DC Turner and DC Gregson. They want information about a job that is being lined up, and they want to know who is supplying her with crack. Finally, Tracy tells the officers what they want to know – with the result that Gregson arrests Colette. 'I'm a hustler,' she protests. 'I don't need to sell crack.' As she arrives at the police station, she sees Tracy in the corridor being taken to the toilet: 'You bitch!' screams Colette. 'Do you hate me now?' retorts Tracy.

Newall arrives at the canal bridge, with Carol and Rose in the back of his car. He tells them to stay there as he gets out and joins Barstow and Hoyle, but Carol jumps out. Newall jumps on Vinnie, who is waiting beneath the bridge with Emma. Newall makes a run for it, but Barstow stops him. Then, Newall carries Emma back to Carol.

When he is interrogating Vinnie at the station, Newall suggests that he killed his uncle after finding out that Curly had changed his will in favour of Carol. Vinnie admits that he went to her house, that he saw his uncle's car there and that he looked through the windows and saw Carol 'walking' for Curly. But he claims that he left immediately to

Rose mistakenly thinks she has found her daughter when she tracks down Sarah Levison in Manchester

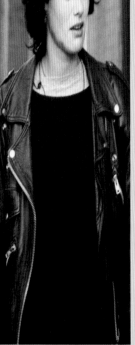

LENA HEADEY
AS COLETTE

Cracking the whip gave up-and-coming actress Lena Headey a whole new perspective on life when she landed the role of leather-clad bondage prostitute Colette in the second series of *Band of Gold* – Colette specialized in sadomasochistic sex, smoked crack cocaine and had a lesbian relationship with teenage hooker Tracy. And finding out how a real-life dominatrix inflicted pain and humiliation on her clients was an eye-opener for an actress who had just finished walking through tropical rain forests in corsets, bustle, petticoats and full Edwardian dress as the innocent heroine of Disney's live-action film version of *The Jungle Book*.

Lena was apprehensive about meeting the prostitute: 'I was quite nervous because I didn't want to appear patronizing in any way,' she said at the time. 'I found it all a bit shocking at first. But we must have talked for a couple of hours. She was 24 and nice-looking, but got into prostitution at 16 when she and a friend decided to see if they could get money for sex. Now she's made lots of money but hates the life – she just wants to get away from it, and says it has made her hate men. She's not gay, but doesn't feel she could have a relationship with a man.

'While we chatted, she was just wearing lacy underwear and pink high-heeled shoes. She was bright and beautiful, but scary and as hard as nails. Every half-hour, she'd see a client, then come back and say: "That was an easy £30," and offer me a cup of tea. It wasn't seedy or glamorous, just ordinary. It was interesting to see how she lived, day to day: she told me that men would lick her carpet, clean her house from top to bottom, cook her dinner – and pay for the privilege. I was shocked to discover that humilia-

tion is a kick for some people. I found it sad.' Lena turned down an offer to watch her in action through a peephole.

Next, Lena went to Soho sex shops with costume designer Nic Ede to get the bondage outfits that would enable her to look the part. Most of the costumes were made of rubber: corsets; bra; G-string; trousers; micro-skirts; short mac; and high boots. They also bought a whip that Lena had to use on her first day of filming.

'I was a bit self-conscious that first day on the set, because I had to whip a semi-naked client,' said Lena. 'I hadn't beaten anyone before, so I hadn't got a clue how hard to do it. I apologized to the actor in case I hurt him. Fortunately, we used a cat-o'-nine-tails, which makes a lot of noise but does not inflict much pain. It was quite odd. You get a strange feeling of power when you have a whip in your hand and you are wearing black leather gear and six-inch stilettos.

'Some days, it was quite cold and the corset was a bit tight, so I'd have red marks on me when I took it off. The costumes were tough but, once I'd grown accustomed to them, it got to be fun.' By the end of the series, Colette was revealed to be the natural daughter of her arch enemy, Rose. And Lena returned for the first two-part story of *Gold*, in which Colette is told the shocking news and has great difficulty in coming to terms with it.

The Yorkshire-born actress, who was just 22 when cast in *Band of Gold*, has appeared in *The Remains of the Day* and in the television films *Clothes in the Wardrobe* and *Devil's Advocate*. She made her mark as an actress when she abandoned her A-levels to make her screen début with Jeremy Irons, in *Waterland*. Although she stripped off for that, as well as for her television roles as an Ecstasy taker in the BBC drama *Loved Up* and the romantic comedy *Fair Game*, Lena has resisted offers from Hollywood producers to shed her clothes for other films after getting noticed for her role in *The Jungle Book*. 'The scripts contained a lot of nudity,' she said. 'That's fine when it's tastefully done. But I won't be there when it's a matter of just spending two hours with your pants off!'

Tracy's pimp, Dez, is released from prison

pick up his fiancée, and that Carol killed his uncle. Convinced by this story, an angry Newall rushes to Carol's house and, calling her a 'lying whore', tries to push through the door, which is held by a chain.

As he arrives back at the station with Carol, Hoyle tells Newall that Vinnie's alibi has checked out. Hoyle complains, as Newall breaks with procedure and takes Carol into the interview room to face Vinnie. She flies at him and the two officers have to pull her off. Then, Vinnie stuns everyone present by asking: 'Who the hell's that?' When he is told that it is Carol Johnson, he says it can't be: 'Carol Johnson's white,' he says. The woman he saw with Curly was not Carol.

By now, Rose has returned to Manchester for her meeting with Sarah, who offers to play the cello for her. Rose agrees, and the young woman's playing brings tears to her eyes. 'That was the loveliest thing I've ever heard,' says Rose after Sarah finishes the piece. But when Sarah says that her father is musical, too, Rose remarks that this is strange, considering that he is not a blood relative. Sarah is confused, so Rose says that she had thought Sarah had told her that she was adopted. Sarah says that she is not – but that she had a sister who had been adopted, who had run away from home when she was 12 and had been put in a children's home. Leaving the house, Rose apologizes, saying: 'I made a mistake.' At the same time, DC Turner looks at Colette's police records in an interview room. She admits to having changed her name from Hannah, after being involved in a sauna that was busted by police: 'Yes, here we are,' says Turner, 'Hannah Levison.'

Episode Five: Love

Tracy's pimp, Dez, leaves prison but Tracy has been reunited with Colette and promises not to go back to him. On finding out that her daughter was a prostitute and might not even be alive, Rose decides to go back on the Lane. Young prostitute Tula is set up to be a decoy on a drugs run, and Anita revels in taking on one of Colette's clients and dominating him.

There are shocks for Rose when she discovers the identity of her daughter, who is still alive, and also for Dez, when Tracy exacts her revenge on him.

When Dez leaves Normanton Prison, Tracy is waiting outside for him: 'I've missed yer,' she tells him. Back at her house, Dez goes to bed with Tracy and then looks in her wardrobe, noting the expensive clothes. 'I don't come cheap any more,' she explains. 'They pay good money for me.' Dez offers to bring Tracy back 'a little lifter', but she tells him she has her own supply.

Meanwhile, Rose is in Manchester, confronting Mrs Levison, who had adopted her baby daughter, Hannah, and looked after her until she was sent to a children's home. Rose starts by giving her a hard time, but Mrs Levison explains: 'She wasn't an easy child – she was jealous of Sarah. In fact, she hated her, and, when Robbie was born, she became even worse. She went completely wild.' Sarah, with Mrs Levison supporting her story, tells Rose that Hannah was taken away to live in a children's home after she had cut all Sarah's hair off and stabbed her with scissors, leaving a wound that needed 27 stitches.

Anita takes a phone call for Colette from Lionel, the corporate solicitor who gave her the advice about George Ferguson after he claimed that he owned half of Scrubbit. Lionel agrees to meet Anita at a hotel after she says that Colette is busy; Anita finishes the call hurriedly as Colette walks up from the cellar. Then Dez comes down from Tracy's bedroom and tells Anita that he wants a key to the house. Later, in the back room, Colette brandishes a bread knife and holds it to Tracy's neck: 'You ever do that again and you're dead,' she screams. Tracy kisses Colette softly, but, as Colette responds, Tracy pulls away from her.

Tula sits with DC Gregson in his car as he complains that Tracy did not give the police any leads on her drugs supplier when she was taken to the station. After a brief argument, Tula gets out of the car and Gregson drives off. Tula sees Tracy in the Lane, and tells her about being pulled in by the police; she also says that she is still interested in taking part in Tracy's planned trip to Belgium.

An emotional Rose returns from Bradford and approaches Brian Roberts, the private detective who gave her the address of Hannah's adoptive family: 'If you'd done yer job properly, you'd have found out they put her in a children's home in Sheffield when she were 12,' Rose tells him, adding that she will not pay his bill.

As Carol opens her electricity bill and gets a shock at its amount, Newall knocks on her door; she is pleased to see him. But Newall tells Carol that he has been suspended for 'abuse of authority, neglect of duty and acting unlawfully'. Carol has little sympathy and he leaves. Rose then returns and, shortly afterwards, DS Hoyle and DC Barstow take her to the station to question her about Curly's murder.

Tracy meets Alf and, when asked about her visit to the police station, explains that she told the police that Colette had supplied her with the drugs. Concerned that she will be under surveillance, Alf tells Tracy that the Belgium trip is off. She says that someone else is willing to go. Later, in the Hustler's Arms, Smiley briefs Tula and gives her an airline ticket: 'You stand by the information desk at the airport, someone'll come over to yer, they'll give yer a kiss and hand you a teddy bear,' he says. Smiley walks out of the pub to his Rolls-Royce and rings Alf on his mobile phone: 'They're hardly gonna be able to miss her,' he says. 'Proper little decoy,' comments Alf.

At the police station, Rose tells Hoyle that she never 'walked' for Curly and says that she has an alibi for the time of his murder: she had been with

> *Dez looks in Tracy's wardrobe, noting the expensive clothes. 'I don't come cheap any more,' she explains*

Brian Roberts. Then she meets Brian, who tells her that he met a policeman when he returned to his house from Sheffield. He tells Rose that he has found out that Hannah ran away from the children's home when she was 15 and went on the game in Leeds with a friend. Rose is shocked.

Meanwhile, Colette is in danger: sadistic punter Karl Weiler – the man who had once bound and gagged Tracy in a hotel room – arrives for a session in her dungeon. He ties her hands behind her back and tells her to say 'Daddy' when she wants him to stop. Then he takes his belt off and hits her back with it hard. He leaves her slumped on the floor with weals across her skin.

Karl Weiler takes his belt off and hits Colette's back hard. He leaves her slumped on the floor with weals across her skin

Smiley visits Brenda Taylor and tells her to claim ignorance if the police ask her about the company that George Ferguson had been setting up. Brian drives Rose to the Leeds red-light district in an effort to find Hannah. On the way, she is in despair at the idea that her daughter grew up to be a hooker, despite having been brought up by a well-off family. Brian suggests that Hannah might have set out to look for her mother. In Leeds, they approach a prostitute who tells them that Hannah worked there for a couple of years with a blonde girl called Colette – but that one of them 'took some bad stuff' and the other was busted. For the first time, Rose realizes that Hannah might not even be alive, and she returns home bitterly disappointed. Later, after drinking several whiskies in the Hustler's Arms to work up her courage, Rose walks out on to the Lane, unbuttons the top of her blouse to show some cleavage and hoists her skirt up, deciding her lot in life is to be on the game.

In a hospital's intensive-care unit, where Joyce's father is seriously ill, Joyce and Steve discuss their guilt about sleeping together. 'It was just a way of being close to her,' he says. 'I don't want you screwing that woman,' says Joyce, referring to Lisa.

When Tracy arrives home and starts cutting up a piece of rock, Colette emerges from the cellar: 'Jesus Christ! What's happened to yer?' says Tracy. Then they work out that Colette's punter was the one who tied Tracy up in the hotel. Then Tracy removes Colette's wrist band to reveal several deep cuts, one of which has become infected. 'Why?' she asks. 'It stops me thinkin' – 'cause I see blood and I know I'm alive,' explains Colette. Tracy says that she wants to love Colette but is afraid that she will hurt her. 'Everybody I have ever loved has hurt me,' says Tracy. 'I won't, I promise,' says Colette, adding that it is her birthday. They then kiss.

Carol visits Newall at his flat, where he has packed a holdall and is planning to leave. She opens a bedroom door to reveal a mixed-race boy in bed and is shocked. 'He's my son,' says Newall. Carol is confused and makes to leave. As Newall tries to stop her, she says the boy's mother must have been black. 'Yer like screwin' black women, do yer?' she asks. 'If I've got the choice, yes,' he replies, before explaining that he was married to the boy's mother – a policewoman – for nine years. As Carol accuses Newall of enjoying the fact that she was a prostitute, a sexual tension builds between them. She tells Newall that he can come to her house later, but he replies that he has no one to look after his son, Liam. She leaves with a smile.

Anita meets Lionel at a hotel, where she plays the role of his dominatrix in one of the rooms: Lionel is wearing women's clothes and down on his knees cleaning out the mini-bar. By now, Anita has drunk her way through it and tells him to go downstairs to the bar and get a bottle of Malibu – she threatens to throw his trousers out of the window if he does not fetch it. The threat spurs Lionel into action, and Anita revels in her new-found power.

On her arrival in Britain after her drugs trip to Belgium, Tula is stopped by a female official as she passes through customs. She is taken to a room, where she claims that the police know about her trip – but she is told that DC Gregson denies any knowledge of her or of the teddy bear, which contains a mixture of cocaine and bicarbonate.

Tracy arrives at the Hustler's Arms, where Dez has been waiting for her. Then Rabbit walks in, and Tracy asks him where he was when she was busted. Dez draws a knife, takes Rabbit outside and roughs him up.

At Steve's house, Lisa tells him that she will be leaving the following day. Then Joyce arrives and is annoyed to find Lisa there. After Steve accuses her of causing trouble, Joyce says that she came to tell him that her father had died. Joyce storms out; he follows and she tells him, 'I just wanted us to be together.' Steve tells her that he is confused and that he will make the funeral arrangements the following day.

Rose is not having any luck attracting the punters on the Lane. Then a car pulls up and she walks over to it. The driver turns out to be Brian, who asks how much she charges: 'Fifty quid!' Rose answers, thinking he will refuse. To her surprise, he takes the notes from his wallet, so she gets into his car – where he shows her a photograph of Colette. 'What do I want to look at a photograph of Madam Leather Knickers for?' she asks. 'She's your daughter,' Brian tells her, explaining that this is a photocopy from criminal records.

Tracy arrives home with Dez and takes him down to the dungeon, where he asks Colette how much she charges her punters. Tracy shows him the manacles, puts them on him and takes the key: 'You've got to know what it feels like, haven't you, if yer looking after her,' she says. Then Tracy draws a knife, lunges at Dez and kills him by slitting his throat.

Tracy shows him the manacles and takes the key…she draws a knife, lunges at Dez and kills him by slitting his throat

Episode Six: Release

As Carol finds out that she has inherited Curly's fortune, the shocked women rally round to cover up the evidence after Tracy's murder of Dez and her confession that she was responsible for Curly and George Ferguson's deaths, too. Steve and Joyce make their peace and Tracy finds her own peace after returning to her father, who admits sexually abusing her.

Colette is sitting in the living room, smoking a cigarette – she is deeply disturbed about what has happened. As she gets up to go into the dungeon, where Dez's dead body is still in the manacles, Tracy – with blood stains in her hair – stops her and kisses her hand. 'He got what he deserved,' Tracy says as she settles down to watch breakfast television, adding that he had not only attacked her with a rock but he had originally picked her up in a railway station, bought her clothes, given her money and told her that he would look after her. Then he gave her drugs and put her on the Lane.

Meanwhile, Carol berates Rose for going back on the Lane, but Rose is still trying to come to terms with the revelation that Colette is her daughter. Anita comes downstairs and gives Carol £40 for rent and electricity, much to her surprise. Then Joyce arrives: 'I need to talk to someone,' she says. Joyce explains that she needs money to bury her father; but she also tells them that Brenda Taylor had admitted supplying the information that had lost Scrubbit the leisure centre cleaning contract; and that she was now being bothered by a man in a Rolls-Royce about a company that George Ferguson had set up.

Carol visits Curly's solicitor, who tells her that his dead client has left £20,000 to her daughter, Emma, and the rest of his estate – money, house and chicken factory – to Carol, so long as she retains his nephew, Vinnie, as manager of the chicken factory and does not return to prostitution. Back at Carol's house, Rose walks in as Anita makes a telephone call to arrange another session with Lionel. Colette is waiting for her: 'I need yer to help me,' she says, before spilling out the story to Rose. Anita, standing outside in the hallway, hears what has happened.

Steve arrives at Joyce's house to collect his children's belongings. She refuses his offer of £120 to help with her father's funeral, saying she will get a loan, have her house decorated and enjoy a holiday. Steve reminds her of what happened to Gina after she had taken out a loan. 'Yer never know, I might pull a nice toyboy,' cries Joyce.

Rose and Colette go to see Tracy, who has barricaded herself in her bedroom by pushing furniture against the door. Eventually they succeed in pushing the door open and find Tracy curled under her duvet in the corner of the room: 'Get out!' she screams.

As Carol arrives home, Newall gets out of his car and tells her that DS Hoyle is 'gunning' for her, because Rose's prints have been found in Curly's car and she believes that the pair of them were responsible for the murder. Newall suggests that Carol start a new life with him in Birmingham. He suggests that she 'hustles' for him on the same terms that she had negotiated with Curly, giving him sex whenever he wants it for £150 a week. 'I'll think about it,' says Carol with a smile, as she walks off towards her house. Inside, Anita tells her about Tracy.

Carol and Anita go round to see Rose as Colette sponges the blood out of Tracy's hair and tells her that they will stop 'hustling and smoking'. Carol tells Rose about the police finding her fingerprints and, when Colette comes downstairs, Carol says that she has had a breakdown herself and knows what Tracy is going through. Colette explains that Tracy was getting revenge on Dez. 'Yer don't think she's done it before do yer?' Carol asks, thinking about George Ferguson. Just then, Tracy appears in the doorway: 'I did it for you 'cause he was tryin' to get the contract off yer,' says Tracy. All the women are shocked. Then Tracy says that she killed her father at Carol's house – but

it becomes apparent that she is talking about Curly. She tells them how she 'walked' for him in black stockings, before going round the back of the armchair and cutting his throat.

The women are bewildered, realizing that Tracy is psychotic. 'It were Curly yer killed,' says Carol. 'No, it were me dad,' Tracy insists. In an attempt to defuse the situation, Rose steps in and tells Carol that it must have been Tracy's father, but this provokes an argument. 'I'm not takin' the rap for her,' says Carol. Then Rose leads Carol and Colette down into the dungeon, where Dez's wrists are still locked in the manacles.

Anita answers the door as the carpenter arrives to do some work for Colette. This gives the women an opportunity to ask him to do some plastering in the cellar to cover up the evidence of the crime. Unnoticed, Tracy leaves the house, walks out into the street and uses her mobile phone to call her father: 'It's me,' she says, realizing he is still alive. 'I'm coming home.'

Meanwhile, Joyce picks her grandchildren up from school, telling Steve that she will not allow them to be in the same house as Lisa and him. In an emotional exchange, Joyce explains that she was worried that Steve would take them back to Blackpool. He says that he is not returning there and would never take the children away from her. The children return home with him.

After Carol has picked Emma up from school, she sees Newall waiting down the road in his car, gets in and directs him to Curly's house. 'She did me a favour,' says Carol as they survey the large house. This alerts Newall to the fact that Carol knows the identity of the killer, but she will not reveal it. Carol makes it clear that she does not need him or the £150 a week that he had offered, but Newall tries to persuade her to go away with him, insisting that they are two of a kind. Carol refuses, but breaks into tears as Newall walks away, out of her life.

As Tracy arrives at her parents' home in Harrogate, her father – who is on his own – is beaming. Then the telephone rings, Tracy answers and hears Rose's voice; she hangs up. 'It was her,' Rose tells the other women. 'She's there. Jesus! She's gonna kill him.'

Back in Harrogate, Tracy's father looks through a family photograph album with his daughter. 'Did you ever do it to Laura?' Tracy asks him. 'You can tell the truth. There's nobody here.' Eventually, he says that he never touched Laura and explains that he abused Tracy because he had been made redundant and his marriage was going through a bad patch. 'You used to look at me sometimes in a certain way,' he says. 'Like you wanted me.' 'I was 11,' Tracy remonstrates. 'You were the only good thing in my life,' he continues, 'the only person who seemed to like me and who'd do what I said. Everything else was slipping away.' With tears welling in his eyes, he tells Tracy that she made him feel powerful, then lowers his eyes in shame. Tracy closes the photograph album and quietly tells her father, 'I'm going to go upstairs now.'

Meanwhile, Rose and Colette are getting a lift to Harrogate in the plasterer's van. When they arrive at the house, Mr Richards answers the door and tells them that Tracy is resting upstairs. They rush past him and Rose finds her in bed, looking pale, young and innocent – with blood trickling down the side of the bed on to the carpet. Rose pulls the duvet cover back to reveal that the sheets are soaked in blood from Tracy's slashed wrist. 'You didn't have to do that,' says Rose in tears, as she strokes Tracy's hair.

A week later, Rose, Carol, Colette, Anita and Joyce are sitting quietly in the Hustler's Arms, reminiscing about Tracy. They hear a car horn outside. 'Taxi's here,' says Carol, who gets up with Rose and Anita to leave for Tracy's funeral. Joyce and Colette say they cannot face it, but Rose persuades Colette to go. 'We'll all be together,' she says. 'Come and say ta-ra to Tracy.' As they walk out of the Hustler's Arms, Rose puts her arm round Colette's shoulder.

WHAT THE PAPERS SAID

'It's hardly the show to watch with your maiden aunt but it's a gritty drama packed high with street cred. And, if you don't mind the fact that all the men are prats, perverts or pimps, then even we humble males can enjoy it.'
Stafford Hildred, *The Sun*

'This is a truly exceptional hour of TV drama in which the emotional lives of the women are given clarity despite a murderous and bloody backdrop.

If you were to wear a hat while watching telly, you would take it off to writer Kay Mellor for including murder, disposal of the body and the search for Rose's daughter in the same episode as two powerful and forbidden kisses...'
JM, *Time Out*

'*Band of Gold* is a compelling drama judged by those street girls whom it judges as true-to-life and as accurate a portrayal as has ever been managed by television.'
David Banks, *The People*

'*Band of Gold* bowed out last night after a stunning second series, with quality acting right up to its bum.'
Lynne Truss, *The Times*

5

Gold

Life for the prostitutes on the streets of Bradford began to change after two series of *Band of Gold*, which highlighted the dangerous environment in which they worked. Various groups were formed to help them, and Kay Mellor was also pleased that her programme had changed attitudes towards prostitution. 'There is not the shame and stigma that was previously attached to it,' she says. 'The most satisfying thing for me is that Trea, the prostitute who helped so much with my research, has come out and admitted to her daughter that she was once a prostitute.'

The debate about decriminalizing prostitution was also widened: 'Criminalization is ludicrous,' says Kay. 'If a woman is up in court and happens to be a prostitute, they have to say that she is known as a "common prostitute", so she is already stigmatized. If she goes for a job, it says on her criminal

Throughout the sequel, *Gold*, Carol's fortune is threatened by Curly's nephew, Vinnie

Carol's half-sister, Lisa (Jayne Ashbourne), falls prey to pimp Charlie (Ifran Meredith), who persuades her to go on the game in the third story of the sequel *Gold*

record that she is a "sexual offender", even though she is a prostitute. This means that a prostitute can never work with children in nurseries or teach in schools. Such jobs will always be closed to her, but all she's ever done is to have sex. It is a deal after all between consenting adults.'

Kay is less sure about whether prostitution should be legalized: 'I'm not advocating that. Legalization would mean that the State would tax the women heavily, and so become the pimp. The women are in dire poverty to start off with, and go on the game to survive. Also, they would be told what to do and young girls would tend to go underground. The first step is to decriminalize prostitution, then we should look at it again.'

When she wrote the second series of *Band of Gold*, Kay Mellor was convinced that it would be the

Kay is less sure about whether prostitution should be legalized: 'I'm not advocating that... the first step is decriminalization'

last. 'I didn't want to do a third series,' she says. 'I was so wrung out after the second series that I had a nervous rash from my hand to my elbow, and my eyes started jumping about. It's purely to do with writing about a dark area, and it's a stressful experience.'

Executive producer Gub Neal had asked Kay about writing a third series while the second was being transmitted. 'I understood why Granada wanted a third series,' she says, 'but I had put so much into the first two series that I felt I didn't want to spoil the work I had done. In the end, I made a deal with Granada that if they would never call anything *Band of Gold* again I would help them do a sequel called *Gold*, so that there would always be 12 episodes of *Band of Gold* and no more.'

The new series was designed to have six

one-hour episodes, just as before, but this time it was divided into three two-part stories. Rose and Carol's exploits were to run through the entire six hours, but three other main storylines – each with new characters – were to run alongside them.

'Each prostitute I spoke to told me I still had to write about various subjects – transsexuals, for example – and I suddenly realized that I was their voice

years until leaving in 1995 to make a television film called *Deep Secrets* for Granada Television. Broadcast in April 1996, a day before the final episode of *Band of Gold*'s second series, *Deep Secrets* starred Colin Salmon as an undercover policeman. Ironically, it was screened on BBC1. When she started work on *Gold*, Gill had plans to develop *Deep Secrets* into a series for Granada.

But Kay's other commitments meant that she could not write the whole series. Instead, she scripted the first two-part story and storylined the other two stories, which were to be written by Mark Davies Markham and Catherine Johnson.

Gill McNeill was given the task of producing the new series. She had worked at the BBC for 16

Her enthusiasm for *Gold* was largely based on her admiration for Kay Mellor, both as a person and as a writer of integrity: 'Kay is a tremendous humanitarian and has great energy,' says Gill. 'She

As a transsexual prostitute waiting for a sex-change operation, Sherrie (Danny Edwards), starts working in the 'toleration zone', endures a beating by nightclub bouncers and is watched closely by Rose's boss, Ed Smithson

Janet Dibley

as Paula

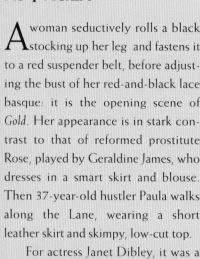

A woman seductively rolls a black stocking up her leg and fastens it to a red suspender belt, before adjusting the bust of her red-and-black lace basque: it is the opening scene of *Gold*. Her appearance is in stark contrast to that of reformed prostitute Rose, played by Geraldine James, who dresses in a smart skirt and blouse. Then 37-year-old hustler Paula walks along the Lane, wearing a short leather skirt and skimpy, low-cut top.

For actress Janet Dibley, it was a traumatic experience to step into Paula's street gear for the first time: 'As I put the clothes on, I was looking at myself in the mirror thinking: "This isn't a joke – this is for real."

'You immediately think about how you look and the fact that your body is exposed. One part of you is criticizing you, saying: "Look at you." Another part is being practical: "It's a job." Afterwards, I took some of the underwear home to come to terms with it. The whole experience throws up feelings about your own sexuality. It was a journey, not just into the character but into my own life. That's what the pleasure – and sometimes, the pain – of acting is about: you find things you don't want to look at.

'A prostitute would have to cut off emotionally from certain aspects of herself. There's a fine line between selling yourself for money and selling yourself in your own personal life. It's all about compromise – what you do in a relationship and how that makes you feel, ' says Janet.

Band of Gold is set in Yorkshire, where Janet spent her childhood. Born in Doncaster, she grew up in Leeds and attended a convent grammar school. While at school, Janet appeared in John McKendrick's play *Rules*, at Leeds University Workshop Theatre, then in Phil Young's *Gas*, which was performed at the National Union of Students Festival in Edinburgh and The Roundhouse, London.

Intent on making acting her career, Janet trained at the Rose Bruford College of Speech and Drama and started in repertory theatre at the then Leeds Playhouse (since renamed the West Yorkshire Playhouse), acting in plays such as John Whiting's *The Devils*, Mary O'Malley's *Once a Catholic* and Tom Stoppard's *Night and Day*.

She went on to play the title role in director Bill Bryden's National Theatre production of *Cinderella*, with a cast including Jack Shepherd, Tony Haygarth and Robert Stephens. She also appeared with the National Theatre company as Miss Sarah in the musical *Guys and Dolls* and performed in the West End as Cherubino in *Figaro* and Constance Wilde in *Oscar*.

Although she appeared on television with Trevor Eve in *A Brother's Tale* and with Diane Keen in *Foxy Lady*, Janet did not find fame until she took the role of crèche worker Elaine in the ITV sitcom *The Two of Us*, in 1986.

After *The Two of Us* finished, in 1990, Janet came up with her own idea for a sitcom. She phoned Alex Shearer, who had written *The Two of Us*, and suggested a comedy about a single mother struggling to bring up her eight-year-old daughter with no financial help from her unreliable ex-husband. The result was *The Gingerbread Girl*, which started in 1993 with Janet in the lead role of Linda.

She then wrote, with Lesley Clare O'Neill, a play called *Daughters or Blood Muckier Than Water*, which they performed it at the 1995 Edinburgh Festival. Janet admits that she never knows what is going to come next. Her main ambitions lie in working in the theatre: 'I would like to work with people such as Tom Cairns and Stephen Pimlott. I love the theatre because it's so consuming, but I also enjoy working on film. *Gold* is the first programme I have done on film since I was in *A Brother's Tale*, which was also made by Granada.'

has given life to two characters, Rose and Carol, who don't just lie down and sleep. They had 12 hours of history and very powerful stories.

'Rose was desperately trying to get into the position in which she was earning money legitimately. She had to prove to herself that she could survive without prostitution, that she had a contribution to make and that she was of value, so that she could tell Colette: "I was your mother. I was a

'Kay has given life to two characters, Rose and Carol, who just don't lie down and sleep. They had 12 hours of history'

hooker, but I got out. I can help you." It takes a great deal of courage for her to confess to Colette in the first hour of *Gold*. In the second hour, you see the beginning of a new relationship. It's very painful and it isn't resolved.

'Meanwhile, Carol's life has changed from hooker to wealthy woman because one of her punters, Curly, left his fortune and home to her. The one thing that Carol had always wanted was

Rose is hysterical as pimp Charlie Wallace (Colin Salmon) – one of the Leeds contingent who have taken over the Lane – pulls a gun on her, claiming that she was responsible for setting him up for his girlfriend Marva's murder

Adam Kotz returns to his role as Vinnie Marshall, Curly's nephew, who became manager of the chicken factory but resents the fact that Carol inherited his uncle's fortune and is determined to wrest it from her.

Judy Brooke, who played James Bolam and Barbara Flynn's child-minder in *The Beiderbecke Tapes* and Paula Maxwell in *Coronation Street*, plays Vinnie's secretary, Julie.

John Ashton, whose longest-running television role was as Chief Superintendent Don Henderson in two series of *Waterfront Beat*, was cast as Paula Graham's husband, Tim, in the first story.

Rosie Rowell, famous for her role as Donna Tucker in five series of *Soldier Soldier*, plays the part of prostitute Maggie in the second story.

Andy Rashleigh, frequently seen on television as a policeman but best known as Colin Arnold in *Albion Market* and Chef in the final days of *Crossroads*, was cast as chicken factory worker Robson in the transsexual story.

Jayne Ashbourne, who acted Carmen in *The Riff Raff Element* and Sarah Madson in *Madson*, plays Carol's half-sister, Lisa, in the final story.

financial security. Cleverly, Kay made Curly's will include the proviso that Carol must stay off the game. Curly's nephew, Vinnie Marshall, was deeply upset about being disinherited, although he took over the running of his uncle's chicken factory. So from the word go there is a revenge story, and Vinnie puts Carol under threat. She does get to enjoy her money for a few scenes, but that soon changes.'

At the end of *Band of Gold*'s second series, Rose and Colette were seen leaving the Hustler's Arms. *Gold* starts with Colette still unaware that Rose was her natural mother. 'Real life isn't so neatly packaged,' says Kay Mellor. 'You don't find out who your daughter is and immediately tell her. People stay with things like that for years out of the fear of rejection. I wanted to explore the situation properly.'

In the elapsed time between the end of *Band of Gold* and the start of *Gold*, Rose had taken a leisure

and tourism course and moved in with Carol, who was by now living in Curly's large house. Rose soon finds herself back on the streets – but this time as an outreach worker who helps prostitutes who have been driven out by residents and moved into a 'toleration zone' created by the council and police: it's a safe area in which they can work, where free condoms and VD check-ups are provided.

As well as developing the stories of Carol and Rose, Kay wrote the outlines of three new stories designed to ensure that the issue of prostitution remained central to the series. 'I went with Geraldine James to a conference in London held by the English Women's Collective,' says Kay. 'It was trying to raise funds for a new office and asked us for help. It had given us a lot of help with research, so it was good that we could give something back.

'When we arrived, we found a church hall packed full of prostitutes and priests: I presume that the priests were there to see what was going on. The prostitutes said that they all thought that *Band of Gold* had been absolutely authentic – I couldn't believe it, and was elated. Each one who spoke told me I still had to write about various subjects – transsexuals, for example – and I suddenly realized that I was their voice. There were whole areas I hadn't even tackled.'

So, Kay came up with ideas for three other major stories in the new series: a prostitute accused of killing her clients; a transsexual; and pimps moving in from outside to take over the Lane after the original prostitutes have moved to the 'toleration zone'.

Mark Strong, who played a detective alongside Helen Mirren in *Prime Suspect* and won heart-throb status for his roles of Tosker in *Our Friends in the North* and Mr Knightley in *Emma* on television, was cast in the first two stories as Rose's boss, property developer Ed Smithson. Janet Dibley, best known as Elaine in the sitcom *The Two of Us*, played ageing prostitute Paula Graham, whose clients were being murdered. Danny Edwards, who made a name for himself as a drag performer in cabaret and in the BBC documentary series *Soho Stories*, played Sherrie, the transsexual featured in the second story, complete with prosthetic breasts. Colin Salmon, who had starred in producer Gill McNeill's television film *Deep Secrets*, as well as acting a detective in *Prime Suspect 2* and Jamaican immigrant Noah in the revival of *Shine On Harvey Moon*, played Raymond Wallace, the pimp, in the final story.

In the first story, the murderer's trademark is to creep up behind the victims and hit them over the head with a brick. 'This presents an amazing problem,' says Stunt Arranger Stuart St Paul. 'The art of

> *'To push an actor wearing stilettos around in a triangle between three men, like a rag doll, could result in him breaking an ankle'*

selling a blow in a stunt is in the set-up. The blow itself is so quick that the eye doesn't take it in. So, if you're not allowed to show the attacker, the blow has to be delivered slightly more slowly than normal, even though it's only a rubber brick. The brick is left in the frame for a fraction of a second after the blow.'

In fact, Stuart was kept busy throughout filming of *Gold*. For a scene early in the second story, in which transsexual Sherrie is attacked by two bouncers in a nightclub toilet after they kick in the door, Stuart had to ensure that actor Danny Edwards, playing the transsexual, did not fall badly and injure himself.

'Little things can turn into big problems if you don't spot them before they happen,' he says. 'For instance, Danny was wearing stilettos. To push an actor wearing stilettos around in a triangle between three men, like a rag doll, could result in him falling over and breaking an ankle – especially if it's someone who is not used to wearing stilettos. So we took Danny's stilettos off, avoided filming his feet and added a soundtrack afterwards.

'We also did a scene in which Paul, who has been summoned by his sister Cathy, gives Vinnie a bit of a pasting. There's a chase down the alleyway in which Vinnie scales a steel gate and Paul picks up a dustbin and throws it at him, bringing him falling to the floor. It was all filmed in a morning: we used a stuntman to stand in for Vinnie so that he could land safely on the ground and not end up hitting the dustbin, which was also coming down.'

The beating of prostitute Helen by men from the factory ends in her being thrown out of a car on to waste ground, after the car has screeched to a halt. Stuntwoman Anna Stacey stood in for actress Louise Atkins during filming of this action scene.

'The problem here was that we had a woman dressed in clothes that didn't cover her elbows and knees, and she had to be thrown out of the back of a car,' says Stuart. 'You can't let an actress do that. It would be very easy to break a wrist or graze some skin. But the double must not show her face, so she either has to turn her back to the camera or put her arm across her face, if it is towards the camera, so that viewers cannot spot that it is not really the actress.

'Also, she could have been thrown out of a moving car, rather than a stationary one, which would have been more dramatic, but that would have changed the character of the men and the character of the abuse. And it would lead to different retribution, which wasn't right for the story.'

There were two more spectacular pieces of action in the final story of the series. When prostitute Ashley is bound and gagged by her pimp,

When prostitute Ashley is bound and gagged by her pimp, Shaun, she escapes by jumping through a window

Shaun, she escapes from a first-floor flat by jumping through a window. 'The added complication is that her hands are tied behind her back,' says Stuart. 'The trick of going through a window head-first is that you have to attack it. If you let the window hit you, it will cut you. So the stuntwoman's job was to head-butt the glass.'

The interiors for a horrifying fire at the end of the series, involving Rose, Carol, her daughter Emma, half-sister Lisa and the pimp Charlie, were filmed at Chorley Fire Station, which is also a training centre for fire-fighters and provided a controlled setting for the production team.

'Arranging it was a bit of a nightmare,' recalls Stuart, 'because I had to put doubles in for all the actors when they were seen in long shot. For Emma, I used an Indian midget called Keiron Shah, who has been in endless films, such as *Star Wars* and *Willow*. On close-up shots, the actors had to be there with flames all around them and it can get incredibly hot and smoky. They all had to be quite brave, but I placed them near doors for those shots

so that they could get out quickly if necessary, and the cameras filmed them very tight so that it wasn't obvious that they were in a different place to the stunt performers. To create the fire, we ran steel tubes down the walls and flamed them with gas, which we could turn up or down. We also pumped fireballs down corridors.'

Carol's new-found home and wealth meant that Production designer Chris Wilkinson had to search for a location for the house that she had inherited from Curly. In the second series of *Band of Gold*, he used Aspenshaw Hall, near Buxton, where exteriors only were filmed. But, because a number of scenes in the new series demanded interior shots, Chris looked for a property closer to Manchester and found a large, late-Victorian house in Altrincham, Cheshire, that was suitable for both interior and exterior shots.

'It gave us a big living-room and hall, huge kitchen and large bedrooms,' says Chris. 'In deciding how to decorate it, I had to take into account that Carol likes bright colours. The costume designer gave her a completely new wardrobe of bright colours and I had to echo that. So I used Caribbean Crush – a bright pink-orange colour – in the lounge, with similar colours and wallpapers elsewhere.'

The Lumb Lane scenes were shot, as before, in Ashton-under-Lyne and the 'toleration zone' was filmed behind the old Express Newspapers building in Ancoats, a short distance from Manchester city centre. And Chris built Rose's office inside an old mill in the same area, with partitions that included windows, so that some of the mill could be seen.

The flat above a tandoori restaurant in Ashton-under-Lyne, used as Anita's flat in the first series of *Band of Gold*, became Paula's flat in the first story of the new series. 'We kept the exterior the same but made the interior seedy: a place in which she would carry out her business with clients,' says

DANNY EDWARDS
AS SHERRIE

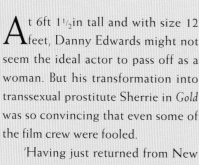

At 6ft 1½in tall and with size 12 feet, Danny Edwards might not seem the ideal actor to pass off as a woman. But his transformation into transsexual prostitute Sherrie in *Gold* was so convincing that even some of the film crew were fooled.

'Having just returned from New Zealand, where I played a transsexual in the film *Heaven*, it was like continuing the role that I had been playing for three months,' says Danny. 'I had no worries about acting that type of character, just excitement about the fact that I was in *Band of Gold*.

'Sherrie's not the brightest of people,' says Danny. 'She's loud, sassy, brassy and offensive – it's all a defence mechanism to hide her own insecurities: transsexuals, especially very tall ones, are extremely insecure about being laughed at in the street. Like a lot of natural-born women, she says she is only going on the game until she has saved sufficient money, but then she gets drawn in.

'To play her, I drew on aspects of my own personality and those of some of my friends. I had to be careful, though, not to alienate the audience by acting too aggressively.

'When the make-up comes off, some actors find it hard to step out of character. And for me it's so nice to be a boy again. Some of the crew called me "she" and treated me like a woman, which was great for the persona. In the nightclub scrape some people were saying, "Don't push her too hard," and asking if I was OK. I was thinking: "I can look after myself and I've done male stunts before but, because I've got these breasts and stiletto heels and nail polish, they are treating me like a delicate little woman." '

Success as a drag artist and playing transsexuals has come after years of acting during which time Danny didn't get the recognition he thinks he deserved. The nephew of actor Rob Edwards and second cousin of former *Crossroads* actress Jane Rossington, he was influenced as a child by mime artist and choreographer Lindsay Kemp, who is best known for erotic productions of ballets and plays such as Oscar Wilde's *Salome*, and often appears in female roles. 'I was always excruciatingly precocious and hyperactive as a child,' says Danny. 'I went to the shows that my family were in and my mother took me to my first Lindsay Kemp play when I was about six.'

He acted in school plays and took ballet and tap-dancing classes. At the age of 12, Danny stepped on to the professional stage as Curio in *Twelfth Night* and Paris's Page in *Romeo and Juliet*, both at the Beck Theatre, in Hayes, Middlesex. A year later, he started performing with the National Youth Theatre and, from the age of 16, trained at the Anna Scher Theatre School.

Theatre work and a few commercials followed until, aged 22, Danny changed direction. 'I took a year out of acting in order to travel, but ended up working in restaurants.

'Then, a job came up singing at Madame Jo Jo's drag cabaret bar in Soho. I had never done drag before but always found it fascinating, thinking of it as an extension of performance. If you can fool an audience completely, that's acting. Men and, sometimes, women can change their gender completely through make-up.'

Danny first achieved notoriety with the BBC documentary series *Soho Stories*, in 1996. Away from acting, Danny's biggest thrill is recording dramas and sitcoms on video when he's away or even when he's in, watching one channel and recording another. 'Then, when I have free time, I lock myself in the flat, get loads of food in, put my answer machine on, ignore the front door and watch videos for four or five days, smoking copious amounts of cigarettes – my idea of heaven!'

Carol and Rose's lives have changed, but they are drawn together once more when prostitute Paula (right) is accused of murder following the deaths of men with whom she has had sex

Chris. 'We put in a bit of sadomasochism gear, blue movies and lots of photographs of herself in scantily clad outfits. Most of the scenes there were filmed at night, so the wallpaper was fairly dark to help with the lighting; the furniture was second-hand and pretty seedy, too.'

Tim, Paula's estranged husband, lived in a semi-detached house. For exterior filming, Chris found a suitable property dating back to the 1930s in Eccles, outside Manchester. Interiors were shot in a studio set up inside a warehouse in Cheetham Hill, which was also used for interiors of Colette's flat in the first story and transsexual Sherrie's flat in the second one. The latter was decorated in red and orange, to give it a surreal feel, and sparsely furnished. Exteriors were filmed at a dilapidated Georgian house in Ancoats.

Charlie, one of the pimps featured in the final story, lives in a flat that was created in the studio at Cheetham Hill. Again, it is sparsely furnished.

Exteriors were filmed at a flat above a disused shop in Ashton-under-Lyne.

GOLD: THE STORY

Episodes One and Two: She's Back

Back on the Lane after marrying a punter but failing to adjust to a 'normal' life, Paula Graham is the police's prime suspect when two of her clients are murdered. Rose finds herself involved when she gets a job as an outreach worker, helping the local prostitutes, and Carol's new-found wealth is threatened by Curly's nephew, Vinnie.

Paula Graham, hard and uncompromising, is back on the Lane at the age of 37 after failing to come to terms with married life and finds herself the target for abuse from vigilantes: 'Whore! Slag! Get back in yer brothel!' they shout. Then someone starts to kill anyone who has gone with Paula: first, married man James Allan, who tries to have sex with her without using a condom; and then DC Simon Mace, after she gives him a 'freebie'.

Meanwhile, Rose, still intent on staying off the game and 'going respectable', applies for a job as a hotel receptionist. But her potential is spotted by Chief Inspector Henryson, who recruits her as an outreach worker on Project Angel under which a joint police–council effort has allowed the setting-up of a 'toleration zone', where prostitutes can work in a safe environment, free of pimps and with condoms supplied.

Carol is wary of Rose's new role, because of the police involvement. She is more concerned with spending her money on expensive designer outfits, and believes that Rose should confess to Colette that she is her natural mother. Curly's solicitor, Mr Chubbs, who has to oversee the conditions of his dead client's will, tells Carol that Vinnie has accused her of going back on the game and supplied photographs of men entering her house regularly. But they turn out to be Carol's decorator and plumber, and she flirtatiously invites Mr Chubbs to visit her.

Rose's first task in her new job is to visit Turton Lane Police Station, where she is shocked to discover that Paula is being held on suspicion of attacking James Allan, one of her clients, who has been hit over the head and is critically ill in hospital. At Paula's flat, Rose discovers her ripped and blood-stained T-shirt in the bin. While she is there, Paula's estranged husband, Tim, comes looking for her.

Rose arranges to meet Colette at the Hustler's Arms, but Rose finds Paula there with DC Mace, who later leaves with Paula for a 'freebie'. And when Colette arrives, she is stunned when Rose breaks the news that she is her daughter. Rose is desperate to explain her reasons for having to give up Colette for adoption, but Colette cannot cope with the revelation. She stands up and, filled with anger, kicks over a table before leaving.

Rose, devastated, walks to the bus stop. A short distance away, DC Mace is struck on the head with a brick as he opens his car door and left for dead. When the police arrive at Paula's flat the following morning, she escapes by jumping from her bedroom window on to the extension of the Indian restaurant below. Rose arrives at the police station to find that several prostitutes are being interviewed – including Colette, who tells Rose that she was probably pleased to get rid of her as a baby and shows no sign of agreeing to her mother's hopes for a reconciliation.

After Carol receives a phone call from a potential punter and finds 'whorehouse' scrawled on her front door, she is certain that Vinnie is behind the campaign against her. So she sprays the word 'bastard' across the bonnet of the Porsche owned by Claudia, his fiancée. But Vinnie is determined to win back his uncle's fortune, and he offers Carol's decorator, Lloyd, a bribe to tell the solicitor, Mr Chubbs, that Carol is on the game.

Rose finds Paula in a building on the nearby industrial estate, and doesn't know whether to tell the police. Paula insists she was not responsible for the murder, and Rose takes her to Carol's house. Shortly afterwards, James Allan dies in hospital.

As Carol is shocked to find out that she has little money left in her bank account, Rose has a plan to establish who is responsible for the murders…

Episodes Three and Four: A Walk on the Wild Side

Rose finds herself with conflicting loyalties when transsexual Sherrie goes on the game in the 'toleration zone', becomes the dangerous obsession of her boss, Smithson, and is witness to a prostitute being attacked. When Vinnie tells social services that Carol is running a brothel, her brother Paul beats him up, and it emerges that Vinnie is siphoning off the chicken factory's profits.

Rose, in her own office in the 'toleration zone', opens her mail to find business cards that read

COLIN SALMON

AS RAYMOND

Pimp Raymond Wallace in *Gold* was a role that Colin Salmon could easily relate to, having grown up in a poor area of Luton, sharing a three-bedroom house with nine others while his father worked in a factory. 'Pimping is not an easy way to get money, but they have nothing else. A lot of them are drug addicts and have to feed a daily habit, which takes ingenuity and effort. If they had self-esteem and opportunity, they could do anything.'

Born in Bethnal Green, East London, to an English mother and a West Indian father, Colin was two months old when the family moved from an East End slum to Luton to live with relatives. 'There were three families and 10 people in the house,' he recalls. 'My strongest memories are the smell of paraffin from the heating – which makes me sick to this day – and the shouting.'

Music provided salvation when his grandfather gave him a cornet at the age of five. Two years later, he joined a Salvation Army band and stayed with it until he reached 15, playing his instrument and singing as a soloist.

Colin's interest in acting began when he started drama therapy, in juvenile centres and psychiatric hospitals. When the Tricycle Theatre, in Kilburn, staged *The Great White Hope*, about Colin's hero, world heavyweight boxing champion Jack Johnson, he busked outside the theatre and was given tickets to see the play. He was 'adopted' by the theatre and, in 1989, given a role in the musical *All or Nothing At All*, about Billie Holliday.

Colin was spotted playing the trombone in the West End musical *Buddy* by Granada Television casting director Doreen Jones. As a result, he made his television acting début in *Prime Suspect* 2 as Det. Sgt Robert Oswalde, who bedded his boss, played by Helen Mirren, and agonized over his identity as a black police officer. Later, he starred as an undercover policeman in Granada's thriller *Deep Secrets*, which was sold to America, and which he hopes will be turned into a series.

Colin also acted Jamaican immigrant Noah, facing racism in London's East End in the 1950s, in the revival of *Shine On Harvey Moon*. 'That was dedicated to my dad and his generation,' says Colin, who is married to Irish painter Fiona Hawthorne and has two daughters, Sasha and Rudi, and one son, baby Eden.

After filming the role of Robinson, MI6 chief of staff, in the new James Bond film, *Tomorrow Never Dies*, Colin jumped at the chance to join *Gold*. Before filming his part, he went to see real-life pimps. 'You can't approach characters without seeing their eyes,' he says. 'I set up a meeting with a pimp in a pub in Chapeltown, which fell through. But I went anyway.

'I wanted to hear them talk, but researching is also about seeing how people move in their world. There was a generational difference: the young guys on computer machines, and the older ones playing dominoes and laughing.

'One older pimp considered himself a lover. He was pleasant and respectful of the barmaid. You could see how people could fall for him. I wanted to know how he started as a pimp. He was with a girl who loved him very much and he fell on hard times, so she turned a trick, which has echoes of the other pimp, Charlie, in *Gold*.

'I wanted viewers to see how Raymond could be magnetic. He has a few heavy scenes where people cross him, but he usually works on a psychological rather than a physical level. He's a lover, not a callous bastard. He's like a father to his girls.

'The pimp I met could be cruel without slapping girls about. There was another, younger pimp, though, who was quite cruel. The locals are very sad about what has happened to the area. That's the pimps' world – that's their business, and it's tragic.'

Rose puts her past to good use by becoming an outreach worker for Project Angel while Carol spends her new-found wealth on designer clothes and decorating the large house she inherited from Curly

'Rose Garrity, Project Manager' and a mobile telephone. Her self-satisfaction is cut short when a gang of men throws a brick wrapped in flaming rags through her window with the inscription 'Slags Die'.

Meanwhile, transsexual Sherrie, dressed up like a Hollywood star, arrives at a nightclub and is noticed inside by Rose's boss, Ed Smithson. When Sherrie emerges from the women's toilets with a male punter, two bouncers grab her and demand a cut of the fee, which she refuses to give them. When she takes another punter to the toilets they follow her and find her in a cubicle performing oral sex. The punter disappears and the bouncers knock Sherrie around until Smithson comes to her rescue and sees the transsexual home.

Carol realizes that her bank account is in the red because, although the chicken factory's sales have increased, profit margins have mysteriously plummeted. At the factory, a group of workers led by Robson and Kevo spend their lunchtime verbally abusing prostitutes outside in the 'toleration zone', before Carol arrives, threatening Vinnie that she will bring in accountants to investigate if the business's finances do not improve. Shortly afterwards, Vinnie phones the local social services department and says that Carol is running a brothel from her house, in which her nine-year-old daughter is living.

As Smithson joins Rose in her office to talk about the previous evening's brick attack, Sherrie walks in asking for free condoms – neither Sherrie nor Smithson acknowledges their encounter at the club. Sherrie then goes out on the 'toleration zone' for the first time and is barracked by the factory workers, along with the other prostitutes. That evening, Maggie is chased down an alley by Robson and Kevo, who brandishes a piece of wood. Later, a battered and bruised Maggie returns to her flat, where Helen is waiting outside with her belongings, having been evicted by her landlord.

Maggie refuses to go to the police, so Helen visits Rose the following day – and Rose tells Chief Inspector Henryson that he must do something. Two social workers visit Carol just before the arrival of her brother Paul, whom she has not seen for many years. Carol suspects that he is gold-digging, but Paul tells her that their mother is ill with cancer and that their half-sister, Lisa, has been particularly good about looking after her.

Smithson, fascinated by Sherrie, starts making phone calls to her and hanging up without speaking. He also watches her perform oral sex with a punter. Rose, trying in vain to persuade Maggie to go to the police, sees Smithson in his car watching Sherrie. When she walks across to him, he invites her to be his guest at a rotary club function.

More violence is meted out by the factory workers when Kevo and Robson start mauling

THE CHARACTERS

Rose Garrity is living with Carol, having taken a leisure and tourism course in an effort to gain respectability and put her hustling days behind her. She applies for a job as a hotel receptionist but is offered the chance to become an outreach worker in the prostitutes' new 'toleration zone'.

Carol Johnson inherited Curly's fortune, detached house in five acres and his £2 million frozen chicken business, to the annoyance of his nephew, Vinnie Marshall. She enjoys spending her new-found wealth on designer clothes and decorating the house.

Colette is still unaware that Rose is her natural mother and continues to earn a living as a bondage prostitute. But she is toying with the idea of moving to London, following the death of her teenage prostitute friend Tracy Richards.

Ed Smithson is a property developer and magistrate who is Rose's boss on Project Angel. Previously married with a young son, he becomes obsessed with transsexual Sherrie.

Paula Graham gave up life on the game to marry one of her punters but cannot cope with 'normal' life and returns to the Lane, aged 37. When her clients start being murdered, she falls under suspicion.

Sherrie, whose real name is Leroy Goodman, is a transsexual who has had hormone treatment to develop women's breasts but is saving for surgery. He goes on the game in the 'toleration zone' and finds himself the object of Smithson's fascination.

Raymond Wallace is a powerful pimp from Leeds who has taken over the Lane. He is the chief suspect when a prostitute is murdered.

Helen in their car. When she bites Kevo's finger, he slaps her face. Then they drive off, screech to a halt and throw Helen from the car. As they get out, Sherrie sees what is happening, picks up a piece of lead piping and runs towards the car, screaming furiously, just as Carol leaves the chicken factory. As a result, Kevo and Robson drive off at speed and Carol phones Rose at the rotary club fund-raiser to tell her what has happened.

An ambulance rushes Helen to hospital, where Rose meets Carol and Sherrie. Then, while being wheeled into surgery, Helen announces: 'I think me baby's coming.' She is taken to the labour ward and gives birth to a baby girl. Carol tells Sherrie that she must identify the attackers, but Sherrie is terrified and leaves. Rose and Carol subsequently fail to persuade Helen to identify them. Later, Sherrie agrees to identify the factory workers in return for a reward and goes to the factory with Carol and Rose: as a result, Robson and Kevo are arrested. Later, Carol plots her revenge on Vinnie, and gets brother Paul to beat him up in an alleyway.

Sherrie arrives home to find Smithson rifling through her possessions after breaking in. As Sherrie bursts into the bedroom and lunges at Smithson, he grabs Sherrie's groin. 'I had to find out, see if you were all there, everything in its proper place,' says Smithson. 'And what do you know, it is. It really is.' What then happens traumatizes Sherrie and leaves a shocked Rose in a dilemma about what to do…

Episodes Five and Six: Tainted Love

With the prostitutes now working in the 'toleration zone', the Lane has been taken over by pimps from Leeds, led by the powerful and dangerous Raymond Wallace. A murder hunt begins when prostitute Marva is found dead and, later, another hustler is badly beaten up by a pimp. Carol's half-sister, Lisa, falls prey to another pimp, who poses a threat to Carol's chicken factory and her daughter.

Rose walks into the Hustler's Arms to find that the pub and the Lane have been taken over by outsiders from Leeds. Gangsta rap pours out of the jukebox and the new clientele – pimps, villains and 'sweetie girls' – have pushed the locals to one side. Armani-suited pimp Raymond Wallace is the centre of attention.

At a psychiatric hospital, a doctor explains to Carol and her half-sister, Lisa, that their mother has taken an overdose because her cancer has made her severely depressed. Meanwhile, the dead body of prostitute Marva is found on a railway embankment by the police. Rose tells Chief Inspector Henryson that she has never met the woman, and Henryson says that he wants Rose to carry on with her job and that the police will find a new sponsor to run Project Angel. Later, Rose tries to speak to prostitutes on the Lane but Raymond warns her off.

Lisa comes home with Carol, who is wary about letting her stay. Later, Carol leaves Lisa in a shopping mall while she visits the chicken factory, and Lisa is approached by Charlie, a pimp from the Lane. By the time she returns, Lisa is sitting in a café with Charlie. Unable to find her, Carol goes home. When Lisa returns, she has an argument with her half-sister, which ends with Lisa calling her a prostitute in front of Emma. Later, Lisa walks out and an agitated Carol shows signs that her cleaning obsession is starting to return.

Helen tells Rose that she had seen the murdered prostitute with the Leeds contingent. Rose, concerned about Helen carrying a heavy holdall so soon after having a baby, takes the bag from her and discovers Helen's daughter, Tia, inside, wrapped in a baby-gro and blanket.

When Rose goes to the police station to tell DI Cooper about the murdered prostitute, the detective tells Rose smugly that she already knows about her involvement with the Leeds pimps. Then one of them, Shaun, takes prostitute Ashley to a flat above a shop. He binds and gags her as he explains that he is running the Lane now, and there are men downstairs, ready to come up. Later, Ashley struggles to her feet and discovers that the door is locked. When she hears footsteps on the stairs, she jumps out of the window, and falls into bushes at the back of the shop, injuring herself badly in the process.

Lisa, now homeless, meets Charlie in the Hustler's Arms and he says that she can live with him. When Shaun walks in, Raymond asks him where Ashley is, but he claims ignorance. Later, police officers, tipped off by false information from Shaun, take Raymond to the police station to question him about the prostitute's murder, leaving Shaun convinced that he will now be running the Lane. Raymond gives Rose a chilling look when he sees her with Inspector Henryson outside the Hustler's Arms.

In hospital, Ashley tells Rose that Shaun, not Raymond, was responsible for what happened to her. The following morning, Charlie wakes up in bed with Lisa and tells her that he is addicted to drugs and needs money. When he threatens to contact his previous 'girlfriend', Ashley, saying that she had gone on the game to pay for his drugs, Lisa insists he must not do so: the pimp has succeeded in finding another woman to work on the streets for him. Hours later, she is on the Lane – but though she jumps into a car with a middle-aged punter she refuses to have sex with him.

Afterwards, Shaun tells Lisa that he runs the Lane now and can claim sexual favours from her, any time he feels like it. He is now her pimp. Later, Charlie finds her huddled up in his doorway. Meanwhile, Raymond is released by the police when Ashley discharges herself from hospital and gives him an alibi. After a shocked Rose discovers that Ashley has left her perfume at the hospital, she and Carol visit Shaun in the Hustler's Arms, and he admits to shopping Raymond, adding also that he bought the perfume for him to distribute to his prostitutes.

Later, at Helen's flat, Ashley tells Rose that 'sweetie girl' Jae had visited her in hospital and forced her to give Raymond an alibi. Fearing for Ashley's safety, Rose hands her enough money to get away to London – and gives her a letter for Colette, who is in London. When she leaves Helen's flat, Rose is grabbed by Raymond, who puts a gun to her head. She thinks he is about to pull the trigger, but Raymond drives off in her van with Rose huddled up in front of the passenger seat.

Raymond accuses Rose of setting him up for the killing of Marva, who was his girlfriend. They get out of the van in a car park, and Raymond points the gun at Rose and pulls the trigger. She becomes hysterical when she finds out that it is not loaded. Rose explains that he had been shopped by Shaun, from whom Ashley escaped by

They get out of the van in a car park, Raymond points the gun at Rose and pulls the trigger. She becomes hysterical

jumping out of a window. Rose then goes to the police station to give her information to DI Cooper. They rush to Helen's flat to find Helen and Ashley are stoned, having spent Rose's money on drugs. Baby Tia is in a carry-cot bawling her head off and there are drug-taking paraphernalia littered across the floor. It is clear to Rose that Ashley will not be going to London.

Raymond drives to the Lane in his jeep, picks up Shaun and takes him to the flat where Ashley was beaten. Once there, Raymond accuses him of murdering Marva and shopping him. Shaun claims not to have known that the dead prostitute was Marva, but this does not stop Raymond from shooting Shaun dead.

Vinnie, having been sacked from his job as manager of the chicken factory, and having pressure put on him by two loan sharks, tries to persuade Carol to bail him out. Lisa and Charlie kidnap Emma in a bid to get their hands on the money they believe Carol has. The chicken factory is the scene of a shattering climax...

6

Putting the Women on the Street

Getting to know the characters and their environment is essential for those who work behind the scenes to try to depict reality in a television drama. Costume designer Sue Peck, who created outfits for all the characters in the first series of *Band of Gold*, was aware of the need to avoid making stereotypes of the characters. 'The producer, Tony Dennis, gave us some guidance, saying that the programme would be filmed in semi-documentary style,' she says. ' Also, Kay Mellor had based the characters on her research and was concerned that they should be portrayed realistically, not as caricatures.' So Sue joined make-up designer Sue Milton and other cast and production team members when they visited Bradford to meet real-life prostitutes.

'Their clothes were extremely varied,' says Sue Peck. 'They could be dressed normally – in jeans,

Making the prostitutes look realistic on the streets was the top priority blouses and macs, for example – or very obviously, exposing a great deal of flesh. I had to find a way to portray our characters that fell between these two extremes. I was also conscious that we were dealing with a sensitive subject and that the working girls we met were very open and helpful about their work, which filled me with a strong sense of obligation to portray them as realistically as possible.

'For instance, the girls either wear very little jewellery or none at all, as jewellery could be stolen or used as a weapon to injure them. And they don't carry handbags, which could make them vulnerable to theft. Most girls put their money in shoes or boots or down their cleavage – a few use bum bags.'

For the second series, costume designer Nic Ede inherited most of the major characters from the first one, but was able to show their development through his costumes. He also came up with a memorable outfit for newcomer Colette, a bondage prostitute. Ray Holman took over as costume designer for *Gold*, in which he was able to reflect Carol's change of lifestyle after coming into wealth, and Rose's new work environment. Also new characters, such as prostitute Paula and transsexual Sherrie, gave Ray the opportunity to design outfits from scratch.

Sue Milton, who has been make-up designer on both series of *Band of Gold* and *Gold*, won the Royal Television Society Craft and Design Award for Best Make-up after the first series was screened. 'When we were planning *Band of Gold*, the subject was entirely new to all of us,' recalls Sue, 'so our visit to Bradford gave us an insight into how the women felt. That helped with the make-up, because we could decide what we wanted to cover up. A few of the women weren't at all interested in make-up, whereas others were much more interested in "putting a face on".

'The girls wear very little jewellery or none at all as it could be stolen or used as a weapon'

'All my preconceived ideas were wrong. Most people think prostitutes use lots of make-up and have love bites. But we found out they did not allow any kissing, and they don't have love bites – just bruises. One of the women we saw had loose teeth and injuries on her legs after being thrown out of a car – it's very common with these women because they get into dangerous situations. Sex for them isn't like the sex that we know.

'There was a look about most of the women we met, and I tried to put it across convincingly: it's tiredness and weariness. They do the work they do for varying reasons, but they've been trapped into it and it often showed on their faces. There were some very beautiful girls as well. There wasn't any particular type. I decided to give all the characters in the programme at least two different looks: the one they have at home; and a "painted" face that they use on the street.'

GINA DIXON

played by Ruth Gemmell

Gina Dixon's clothes had to reflect the fact that she was a young mother struggling to make ends meet after splitting up from her husband, Steve. Sue Peck, therefore, bought inexpensive-looking outfits and tried to reflect the characteristics of some of the real women of the region.

'In every city, there are a variety of second-hand clothes shops that stock ladies' and gents' clothes from all walks of society,' says Sue. 'These are invaluable when creating because they reflect the taste of the area you are trying to create: Manchester has one such shop, which provided me with various characters' outfits, including Gina's black-and-white suit, which she wore when she was selling cosmetics.

'Because of her lack of money, I suspect that Gina might well have bought her clothes from a catalogue. But when she became a working girl, Gina had to adapt her wardrobe – having seen how Carol dressed to attract the punters, she emulated that look by using her short black skirt turned over at the waist to reveal more leg, along with a reveal-ing black vest top, or she wore a black, figure-hugging lycra dress, possibly borrowed.'

Gina was also given two make-up looks by Sue Milton. 'She had an unmade-up look for when she was at home and another for when she went out selling cosmetics – this one was nicely applied so that she looked pleasant,' says Sue.

'When she tried to fit in with the prostitutes, I felt that she would look at them, ask herself what she should do and decide to put a lot more make-up on. I tried to make her look the way people think a prostitute should look, so she wore brighter colours on her eyes and loosened her hair. She had purple eye make-up and blusher. But Gina never reached the tired look – because she ended up being killed.'

Gina, hard-up and influenced by Carol, went on the streets in a skimpy skirt and black vest top

ROSE GARRITY

played by Geraldine James

The Mother Hen of the Lane, Rose eventually gave up competing with younger prostitutes and came off the game, so her clothes had to change. 'Rose started off as the classic tart, with everything worn very tight and without much taste,' says Sue Peck. 'She wore stockings, black high heels and a short, shiny, old-fashioned gold mac. Rose was in a time warp – the 1970s – and hadn't updated the look. She didn't have much money, but didn't feel it was necessary anyway after being a prostitute for so many years, because she had her regular clients.

'She also had a leopard-print skirt worn with a wide, black plastic belt, as well as an outfit of black plastic trousers, which were cheap and very uncomfortable, and a black, fine-knit jumper, belt-ed in tightly at the waist, with a very wide neckline that would fall off the shoulder quite easily.

'When she left the Lane and went to London, Rose threw away her shiny mac at the railway station. It was like throwing away her past. In London, she went on a business course, so I put her

While on the game, Rose favoured tight-fitting, revealing clothes, but her look was rooted in the 1970s

trying her best to be respectable, but she spent so many years on the game that she cannot help herself,' says Ray. 'She was so used to showing off her body that she still does it subconsciously. She will wear a belt to show off her waist, for example, and always has a fairly low-cut top and short skirt. But they're always very respectable compared with those she wore in the first series.

'In this series, she begins in fairly subdued colours but moves on to brighter colours after she starts her job. By episode three, she feels that she is more in charge. And from her time as a hustler she knows how cold it is at night and realizes that she doesn't need to dress like that now, but she can't help herself.

'She's becoming more practical in her dressing, but her version of practicality involves tight trousers and high heels, not thermals or a winter coat. But I've found her a new green raincoat, in a similar vein to the gold mac worn in the first series but much smarter than it, although it's still cheap.'

Sue Milton completely transformed Geraldine James's off-screen look to turn her into Rose when *Band of Gold* began. 'With Rose, I used colours that I wouldn't choose for Geraldine herself: bright colours for her lips and eyes,' she says. 'I tried to make her look tired by darkening the eyes, and we put blonde highlights into her hair to make her look brassier.

'When Rose went to London, tried to improve herself and shed her past, we softened her hair, giving it a warmer look by using a golden rinse, and reduced her make-up. We gave her more flattering lipsticks in brown-pinks. But when Rose returned to Bradford, she joined the others in bidding for the leisure centre cleaning contract, so I had to work out what her version of looking good would be: she was doing her best to look respectable, but never really succeeded. We made the lipstick bright again and

in more flowing clothes and tried to take her as far away as possible from the old Rose. She had baggy jumpers and longer skirts that hid her legs, whereas before she wore anything that flaunted them.'

In the second series of *Band of Gold* Rose worked in the cleaning co-operative and tried to stay off the game, and costume designer Nic Ede continued to reflect Rose's move away from her street clothes. 'She made an effort to appear more mumsy and less tarty,' says Nic. 'I made her look more mature as she tried to find respectability and searched for her daughter, but Rose never managed to get it quite right.'

Ray Holman continues the theme in *Gold*, when Rose lands a job as a project worker helping the prostitutes who have been moved from the Lane to a 'toleration zone'. 'Rose is always

'In the second series Rose worked in the cleaning co-operative... appearing more mumsy and less tarty'

put her hair up to one side, not using the golden colour any more but dulling her hair. Rose didn't use much lipstick, going in for a more natural look, but we still kept her looking tired, because that was part of her.

'In the second series, Rose went through traumas as she looked for her child, so I simplified her look. But I brightened her hair for *Gold* because I felt she was coming back home: she's back on the Lane, although she's working to help the women. So we went back to having curls in her hair, which would help her to fit in with them. The make-up is also simple, with pink lipsticks, for example, apart from when she goes for the job interview. The tiredness is not as evident this time, because she's living in a more comfortable environment with Carol.'

CAROL JOHNSON

played by Cathy Tyson

For the first series of *Band of Gold*, Sue Peck dressed Carol on the basis that she was, above everything else, a mother who wanted a nice home and everything paid for without hire purchase.

'There was a very clear definition between her home and working clothes,' says Sue. 'At home, she would wear baggy T-shirts and jeans – not to look drab but to appear the opposite of how she did in her figure-hugging working clothes. There were scenes in which she picked up her daughter, Emma, from school and so didn't wear her tart's gear. Her street clothes were simply for practical purposes. She had a good figure and dressed to attract the punters, so Carol wore very clingy lycra dresses with short bomber jackets, usually with a black bra underneath.

'One of the women I met in Lumb Lane said that prostitutes dressed according to their mood. Sometimes, they feel they can dress more over-the-top. This particular prostitute wore high-leg,

Carol's figure-hugging outfits suited her good figure, and she dressed specifically to attract punters

black, patent leather boots, and I decided to put Carol in black suede boots that went above the knee and had high heels.

'Carol, I believe, would have had a variety of specialist garments and equipment for use in her work because of her clients' individual tastes. For example, the dress she wore for Councillor Baker was of black plastic, with very revealing lacing at the sides. And when she "walked" for Curly, she donned a short salmon-pink dress with black bra and suspenders. Curly's particular fetish required her to wear five-denier black seamed stockings and high black patent shoes, which he provided for her.

'During the shooting of these "walking" scenes, a number of these packets of stockings were needed because Curly was seen opening them. Not surprisingly, finding these particular type of stockings proved somewhat difficult in the summer of 1994. But costume people love these kind of challenges!'

In the second series, Carol was no longer a prostitute but resumed 'walking' for Curly. Nic Ede decided that she would dress with more finesse: 'We put her in Next clothes but tried to make her look a little more downmarket,' he says. 'We also went for outfits with softer colouring as a subtle means of depicting the change in her character. My favourite was a dusky pink skirt and sweater, worn with a brown blazer on her trip to see Curly's chicken factory.'

The change in Carol's outfits was more dramatic for *Gold*, after she had inherited Curly's fortune. 'Carol has the money and gained confidence through it,' says costume designer Ray Holman. 'She can go into any shop and buy anything she wants. But would she? Versace can be very intimidating – it's not what she has grown up with. Also, we are limited by the fact that Carol lives in Bradford. The nearest place she can get Versace is in Harvey Nichols in Leeds, but there are lots of shops and boutiques around that sell fake Versace, which is what she buys.'

Sue Milton believed that Cathy Tyson's hair was the key to getting the look right for Carol. 'I felt that a woman could show her sexiness by the way she wears her hair,' she says. 'When I went to Lumb Lane, I found that all the women had something the punters could recognize, whether it was an item of clothing or their hair. Cathy had quite long hair at the time, so I wanted Carol to have "big" hair and created that effect by using Cathy's own hair and adding hairpieces.

'She had two separate make-up looks: at home with her daughter, she hardly wore any make-up and had her hair tied back into a plait or a ponytail; when she went to work, we pulled out her hair to make it big and gave her bright red lipstick. She didn't wear eye shadow, but I made her look tired all the time because her life was tough, and I felt this would show in her face.

'There was a third look for Carol, for the time when she became obsessed with cleaning and had a nervous breakdown. I gelled her hair down and pulled it tightly into a bun. That was to tie in with the image of cleanliness – she couldn't stand hair about her face. The clean, neat look was in stark contrast to her look when she was working as a prostitute. As Carol's nervous breakdown progressed, I made her eyes look more and more tired until she became quite baggy-eyed.

'For the second series, we decided that Carol wouldn't use "big" hair because she was off the game and still recovering from her breakdown. Her look was otherwise the same as before, except she didn't appear as tired because she was getting better – at least on the outside.

'By the end of the series, she had inherited Curly's money. So, for *Gold*, we felt she would show her wealth and femininity. We went back to big hair because she has confidence in herself.

'In the second episode, when she is spending money and pampering herself, Carol decides to have her hair styled. She has it trimmed slightly, with a softer curl and bright orange put into it. As the series progresses, the bigger hair returns.'

ANITA BRAITHWAITE

played by Barbara Dickson

Kept-woman Anita, who was originally having an affair with George Ferguson while renting out her spare room to the prostitutes, gave Sue Peck the chance to have a bit of fun, because Anita brought comic elements to the story and had rather dubious tastes.

'When I first read the script I felt that I knew Anita,' says Sue. 'She dressed to please her lover, George, who gave her money and jewellery. She lived in a dream world, seeing herself as an ex-film star in the style of Norma Desmond in *Sunset Boulevard*: spending her days looking through magazines and painting her nails, waiting for George to visit.

'Her clothes and jewellery reflected this dream-like existence: taste and style were not an issue for her. She had it and would flaunt it! And her style hadn't changed since the 1980s. Her clothes would have been fairly expensive, bought from small boutiques, but her co-ordination was somewhat lacking – shoulder pads and appliqué on every outfit. She didn't know when to stop. And Anita wouldn't possess a pair of flat shoes! You could always tell when she was coming by the sound of her high heels and the tinkling of her many bracelets, which were a nightmare for our sound man.'

In the second series, Anita does not turn to prostitution but finds that she can earn money by becoming dominatrix to Lionel, one of Colette's bondage clients, without having to sell her body. For a scene with him at a hotel, Nic Ede dressed Anita in an electric-blue 'power' suit'. 'It was a bit *Dynasty*,' he says. 'I searched high and low around Manchester. And when I finally found this great suit, I decorated the lapels with beads and sequins, having inherited Anita's fondness for beading and embroidery from the previous series. Apart from that suit, though, Anita hadn't really changed – she was still vulgar!'

Sue Milton decided that Anita would have found a look that suited her and then never updated it. 'Anita had to fit in with the prostitutes and with George, so there had to be an attractiveness to her from both of those angles,' says Sue.

'Anita wore far too much make-up, as some women of her age do, and chose the wrong colour foundations. I went for an orange foundation and deliberately left a line round her neck, finishing the make-up round the chin. Anita had a tiredness to her, not for the same reason as the prostitutes, but because she was hanging around with those nocturnal people. Sometimes, she wore no make-up at all.'

When Anita was hospitalized after George drove at her in a hit-and-run incident, Sue had the opportunity to apply bruises and cuts to Barbara, who performed the subsequent scenes in a neck brace.

Anita's 'ex-film star fantasy' existence was reflected in her ill-matched outfits and jewellery

TRACY RICHARDS

played by Samantha Morton

Teenage prostitute Tracy gave Sue Peck the chance to be daring in her choice of costumes for actress Samantha Morton in the first series. 'Her clothes were quite risqué,' she says. 'At first, Tracy was seen flaunting her body in tight white hot-pants, a halter-neck top, a little white bomber jacket and fishnet tights. There was no sophistication about Tracy. Rose and Carol knew what turned men on, but Tracy was so young that she only knew what her pimp, Dez, told her.

'Tracy's clothes were really fun to do. She also had a black crop-top with white trim and lots of shorts and very short skirts. One of the skirts was made of denim with leather fringing that made Tracy look really sexy as she moved.'

Going to London, getting into the club scene and earning good money as a prostitute meant a transition for Tracy that Sue reflected in her clothes. 'The first time we saw her in London, she was wearing a tight-fitting designer leather jacket that would have cost a lot of money,' says Sue. 'She also had black leather boots and a black dress with fringes that moved as she did. By now, her naïveté had gone and she was earning enough money to pay for the flat that she was now sharing with Rose.

'Another outfit that Tracy wore in London was a long, figure-hugging silver frock with shoestring straps, worn without a bra. It was the sort of outfit that would stand out in club lighting.'

Nic Ede particularly enjoyed creating Tracy's costumes for the second series, in which the character enjoyed the trappings of the wealth she was making from prostitution. 'For a party at drugs baron Alf's penthouse, Tracy had the most incredible halter-neck, fully beaded evening dress,' he says. 'And, for her entrance, she wore a studded silver-blue Gaultier jacket over it. It delivered the message that she had spent a massive amount of

Tracy's risqué clothes included this black crop top with white trim and shorts, revealing plenty of flesh

money on her clothes. She was much harder in that series, and knew where she was going.'

Because the *Band of Gold* team had met prostitutes who work during the day in Lumb Lane during their initial research, Sue Milton returned one evening with location manager Jeff Bowen to find younger prostitutes there. 'They looked as if they were on drugs,' she recalls, 'and I tried to bring that into the character of Tracy because she was into drugs.'

Sue decided to give Samantha Morton a wig for the role and put Tracy through several different make-up looks in the first series. 'Samantha has short, light-brown hair, so we had a bleached wig of yellow-white blonde made for her,' says Sue. 'It was long hair made to look as if Tracy had bleached it herself, so it had roots in it and was broken at the ends.

'Tracy wore quite a lot of make-up. During the early part of the first series, she wore very strong, black eye make-up. Then, she ended up in hospital and returned to her parents. For that part of the story, I made her very plain, using very little make-up but I still gave her a tired look. I used the same wig as before, but styled it completely differently, to give her a young, vulnerable look.

'When Tracy went to London with Rose, I had another wig made for her: it had a bob-cut, and she began using dark grey around her eyes and deep red lipstick to look more sophisticated. This was because Tracy was quite clever, and would have picked up the new fashions on the London scene and immediately fitted herself into them.

'The second series continued that look, but I showed the drugs side of her life: Tracy's skin deteriorated as spots showed and her skin acquired a pallor. I also showed that deterioration through her hair's lack of cleanliness, and I also had black contact lenses made for Samantha so that her eyes would look drugged.'

COLETTE

played by Lena Headey

Nic Ede visited several bondage prostitutes in Manchester to help with his research for Colette, who was introduced in the second series of *Band of Gold* and who was eventually revealed to be Rose's natural daughter. He also went to London sex shops with actress Lena Headey to buy the bondage gear necessary for the role. 'We had wonderful help from shops in Soho,' says Nic 'and I created Colette's image based on what the owners of the shops told us was actually used in the sadomasochists' world.

'Colette had a black rubber corset with buttons down front and a collar, but the problem with dressing Colette was just how far we could actually go. We had to tone things down a bit, so we decided to lengthen the corset a little and gave it less cleavage. We also gave her fewer studs and generally tried to make her appear less blatantly sadistic.

'As well as the corset, Colette had very short micro-skirts in patent leather and a black shiny mac with a nipped-in waist that flared over the hips. She had very little of a normal wardrobe, but would be seen hanging around in a T-shirt and jeans when she wasn't working.'

Costume designer Ray Holman gave Colette similar outfits in *Gold* but aimed to make her appear more sexy and less hard. 'I decided to use the rubber gear, but had a pair of chaps made specially for her in a scene with a client who is very much into cowboys,' says Ray. 'She is wearing a G-string underneath, and the chaps do the job of showing off her bottom.'

Sue Milton also met a bondage prostitute during her preparation for the second series. 'She was 25, but looked about 10 years older than that,' says Sue. 'It's the lifestyle and the drugs that do that. As with the others, I created a tired and pale look for Colette, but I didn't want her to appear as if she wore make-up. We had two different hair looks for her. When she wore her rubber gear and was working, Colette's hair was gelled back tight to give a very hard look. When she wasn't working, we loosened it.

'The character also had a lot of cuts on her arms because she tried to mutilate herself. We gave her tattoos that related to bondage, drawing them on in ink, and gave her a ring through her nose, to make her look harder.

'As with Samantha Morton, we had black contact lenses made for Lena to show how the drugs were affecting her. Apart from that, though, Colette's appearance doesn't really alter significantly in *Gold*.'

PAULA GRAHAM

played by Janet Dibley

Paula Graham, featured in the first story of *Gold*, presented costume designer Ray Holman with the opportunity to give actress Janet Dibley a distinctive look.

'She's a new character and the clothes are completely my creation,' says Ray. 'Paula is hard, and returning to the Lane after a short-lived marriage. She's a hustler in her late thirties, into stockings and suspenders and basques, and has sex industry shoes. But, because of her age and the fact that she was at her height on the Lane in the late 1980s, I've taken her look back to that time.

'When I read the script, it started by saying that Paula was getting dressed and putting on pierced diamante earrings. A basic prostitutes' rule is that

Paula's clothes, including a red lycra crossover dress, are firmly rooted in the 1980s

they don't wear pierced earrings because the punters can pull them. And they don't normally wear expensive jewellery – although they do wear a lot of rings. However, they do their best to show off their bodies, so they generally wear tight clothes that are sexy and short. Also, prostitutes don't wear tights – only stockings with hold-ups or crotchless tights so that the punters can get at them. The point about Paula breaking the earrings rule is that she is going to a hotel room to see a punter whom she knows well and can feel safe with.'

Ray created five costumes for Paula and even more sets of underwear. 'I've never bought so much underwear in my life,' he says. 'Janet Dibley took some of it home and learned to put on the suspenders and stockings. But, for most of her second episode, Paula wears a pair of jeans and a see-through top. The character was supposed to have a big bust, but Janet doesn't, so I've had to pad her boobs out.'

One of Paula's most notable costumes is a short, orange leopard-print jacket with a tight cream top and red-and-black basque showing through from underneath; a big bronze jewelled belt, a tight black lycra skirt, black stockings with suspenders, a chain on her left ankle and huge gold stilettos, as well as diamante earrings, a belted chain round her neck and rings on her fingers.

Ray also designed an outfit for the scene in which Paula takes part in a karaoke evening at the Hustler's Arms. 'It's absolutely outrageous,' he says. 'There's a red lycra crossover dress, very short with a deep cleavage and really tight round her bottom, worn with a black leather jacket, a red basque, stockings, big red stilettos and big 1980s clip-on earrings.'

Although Paula was an older prostitute, Sue Milton saw the comparisons with Rose in the first series of *Band of Gold*, but she had to portray a different person. 'Older prostitutes such as Paula are aware of all the competition from younger girls, so they try to make themselves as attractive as possible and stand out,' says Sue. 'We gave Paula quite a striking image, starting with a very distinctive hair-style, which has height to it, and strong scarlet lipstick. Janet has piercing blue eyes, but we had to age her and make her look tired, so I put black around her eyes.

'The key to it is making her look attractive but thinking what's underneath before applying the make-up. Paula has bruises on her arms, which is an everyday occurrence for prostitutes. Also, a punter bites her lip, so I used dried blood to represent that.'

SHERRIE

played by Danny Edwards

Dressing a transsexual character presented Ray Holman with particular problems when he was working on *Gold*. 'This has rarely been done in television drama,' says Ray, 'so I went to pubs in Manchester's "Gay Village" with Sue Milton to find out the differences between gay drag, which is gay men dressed up as women and can be very "glam", transvestites, most of whom are straight men trying to look like women, and transsexuals, who want to be as womanly as possible in a natural way.

'Psychologically, transsexuals are women, so they don't feel they have to put sequins on. They want the woman's shape and make-up, and want to dress as women as naturally as possible. From our research, we realized that we had to portray our transsexual as naturally as possible, not camp and with no "glam". In fact, it was very difficult to spot transsexuals, but what gives them away is their hands.'

'The producers wanted Sherrie to be sexy, exotic and vulnerable,' says Ray. 'So they decided to cast Danny Edwards, who is 6ft 1½in and has size 12 feet. My job was to make him look like a trans-sexual hooker. I couldn't change his height, but I had shoes made that looked as if they were high heels but weren't, and I put the other women in higher heels so that he wouldn't tower above them.

Wrap-around tops meant Danny Edwards, as transsexual Sherrie, needed to wear silicone breasts

'When Danny and I went to a costume-hire company, I was planning to dress him with a bra, stuffed to appear as if he had breasts. But, because of the nature of the costumes that we chose, such as wrap-around tops and short skirts, I decided to use silicon breasts instead.

'These are very expensive and have convincing nipples, which show through the tight tops. The glue used to put them on every day is also expensive, but we realized that with revealing costumes and a lot of action in the story – when Sherrie is running down the street, for example – a padded bra wouldn't work. We didn't do anything about Danny's waist because the character had so many physical scenes to do that it would have restricted Danny as an actor. The aim was that, for the first 10 minutes, you're not quite sure whether she is a man or a woman.

'I created several different looks for Sherrie with the costumes. When she is seen in a nightclub, she is looking very feminine in a short, tight, red velvet dress with crossover top, an organza coat and black suede stilettos.

'When she's working as a prostitute in the "toleration zone", the first outfit we see Sherrie wearing is a pink, fun-fur coat with a tight, black skirt of crinkled lycra, a silver snake-print top and knee-length buff-colour boots. Then, she wears a much more exotic outfit of a purple, swing coat, a crossover pink top, a little black skirt with a flower pattern and the same boots as before.

'Later, there is a very dramatic scene in which we needed a dress that would tear easily. I found a black stretch nylon dress with pink flowers and a matching crossover top.'

Sue Milton's challenge was to make Danny look convincing as a woman. 'I wanted the character of Sherrie to have her own long hair,' says Sue, 'so I had a wig and a hairpiece made for Danny that looked like the character's own curly hair after it had been straightened. I felt this was more in keeping for a transsexual than to have Sherrie using synthetic wigs.

'I had to use a make-up base to cover Danny's skin completely and to give me a blank canvas on which to work. Then I used highlighting and shading to create a feminine face. For Sherrie's working look, I used heavy eye make-up, two sets of false eyelashes, lots of blusher and strong lipline and lipstick. Pinks made Danny look more feminine, so I used pink-toned lipstick and added pink to the eye make-up. I also used strong pink nail polish.

'To depict Sherrie's decline, I changed the skin tone. I still had my blank canvas to work on and I decided to give Danny a feminine face, but without looking made-up. I could then make Sherrie look distressed or tired by creating shadowy eyes and bags.

'I knew that Ray Holman and I had succeeded when Danny was queuing for lunch one day and one of the security men commented to his colleague, "She's the best one we've had up to now." He had no idea that Danny was a man!'

THE FUTURE

Band of Gold has been so successful that the series has been sold around the world. As Gold went into production in the spring of 1997, Kay Mellor travelled to Los Angeles to discuss an American version of the programme called LA Story: a co-production between Granada Television and the ABC network, featuring an all-American cast in the story of a hustler and another woman teaming up to become private detectives. This is just one of many projects with which Kay has been involved since winning acclaim for Band of Gold.

After the first series, Kay scripted the Granada television film Some Kind of Life, the story of a man who suffers a serious head injury on his son's birthday, which premiered at the London Film Festival. She has also adapted Charlotte Brönte's Jane Eyre for LWT and written Girl's Night for Granada.

Other projects, including plans for Kay to direct two films of her own scripts, mean that she is unlikely to write another complete series of her best-known drama. 'If Gold is to have a life beyond me, it has to live without me, because I can't keep on,' she says. 'I'm not saying I won't write any more episodes and I'd like to steer it. If there is a further series, maybe I could write the first two episodes or the last two and probably storyline the others.'

She recognizes that the success of Band of Gold is a result of 'telling it like it is', as prostitute Trea urged her to do. 'The audience are grown-up people, and you should ever underestimate their intelligence,' says Kay. 'I find so many people in our business do. They say the audience can't take this or wouldn't like that. Would I ever have written Band of Gold had I been worried about it?

'If you dare to give them something that is a cod, because you think, "This will be funny or sensational," that's when you're in dangerous territory. If you can honestly put your hand on your heart and say: "This is real, I know this," they will be with you, no matter how awful the subject is. That's how you learn. You see life and you learn.'